PRAISE FOR BA

Into the current discussion of Christian use of the classical views of vice and virtue, Michael Fieberkorn inserts the witness of Martin Luther. Luther sketched the human life lived in obedience to God in biblical terms. He found that the classic views of vice reinforce biblical condemnations of transgressions of God's design for humanity. The classic list of virtues served Luther less well, for he relied on the Ten Commandments and Paul's lists of gifts or fruit of the Holy Spirit to set forth the life to which God calls His human creatures. Fieberkorn's presentation of the Wittenberg reformer's proclamation of the Christian life, anchored in the First Commandment's fearing, loving, and trusting in God above all things, invites careful consideration and will help believers in the battle to mortify the flesh as they seek support and guidance for life in a turbulent and tempting world. Reflection questions make this not only a good read but also a practical tool for discussion.

Rev. Dr. Robert Kolb, professor of systematic theology, Concordia Seminary, St. Louis

Pastor Fieberkorn has done a great service to the church in writing a relevant and accessible book that addresses the challenge of Christian living in a fallen world. His treatment of vice and virtue, rooted in the writings of Luther, provides practical guidance for the church and the individual Christian. Like we find in Luther's catechisms and Paul's epistles, Fieberkorn contrasts the old way of life that seeks to serve oneself with the new life in Christ that flows from our identity as baptized children of God. The reflection questions at the end of the chapters make this a great tool for group studies in congregational settings. This is a brief and insightful work that helps the reader understand sanctification from Luther's writings.

Rev. Dr. R. Lee Hagan, president, Missouri District, The Lutheran Church—Missouri Synod

The battle is real because sin is real. Likewise, the victory is real because victory has been won and given in Christ. With a pastoral mindset, Dr. Fieberkorn shows Luther's reworked use of vice and virtue and their usefulness in our daily lives as the baptized. Presenting a distinctive Lutheran voice in the virtue ethics discussion, he shows this move from philosophical virtue ethics in the Aristotelian understanding to distinctive Christian virtues informed by the Ten Commandments and the fruit of the Spirit. These flow from faith and are lived in love toward the neighbor in very practical ways in the daily life of a Christian.

Rev. Andy Wright, STM, senior pastor, St. John's Evangelical Lutheran Church, Topeka, Kansas

Dr. Fieberkorn has gifted the church with practical handles on biblical sanctification. No longer are we left with ambiguity regarding our soul's battlefield. The Holy Spirit leads us to know and experience Christ's virtues, countering the vices of sin, the world, and Satan. Fieberkorn demonstrates that Luther's theology held to Christ's Word (for example, the Ten Commandments and the fruit of the Spirit) to teach the results of our baptismal union with Christ. This is a delicious read, full of application and insight on how to live as Christians in the world today.

Rev. Dr. Alfonso Espinosa, senior pastor, St. Paul's Lutheran Church, Irvine, California, and author of *Faith That Sees through the Culture*, *Faith That Engages the Culture*, and *Faith That Shines in the Culture*

BATTLE
OF THE
SOUL

LUTHER REFORMS VICE AND VIRTUE

MICHAEL T. FIEBERKORN

Published by Concordia Publishing House
3558 S. Jefferson Avenue, St. Louis, MO 63118-3968
1-800-325-3040 • cph.org

1 2 3 4 5 6 7 8 9 10   32 31 30 29 28 27 26 25 24 23

To all those who over the years have shaped my understanding of the Christian faith and instilled within me a love for theology and the church

CONTENTS

FOREWORD

We are saved by God's grace through our faith in Jesus Christ alone: *sola gratia, sola fide, solus Christus*. God does it all. We know this and rightly treasure the sweet Gospel truth at the center of our Christian confession and life. The centrality of God's gracious work of salvation is good and right and animates and shapes all that we preach, teach, and practice as Christians.

But now what?

Some suggest there is nothing else to say, that once the Gospel has been declared and received then everything else pretty much takes care of itself. But the Bible and Christian teaching point in a different direction. The truth is that, basking in the warmth and light of the Gospel's glorious truth, we are now to do what the Bible tells us to do: embrace God's continuing work in our lives as His Holy Spirit daily leads and shapes us to live as the forgiven, holy people He says we are. Now that we have the Gospel, we get busy doing the work of living like saints.

And it is work. It is work because while our old, fallen human nature may have been drowned in Baptism, that corrupt, rotting, old nature—that old Adam—refuses to stay dead. With embarrassing regularity, he leaps back to life and with breathtaking power wreaks destruction in our lives and the lives of those around us. The *peccator* that still lurks in each Christian is a monstrous opponent who does not fight fair and does not fight alone; he has the rest of the fallen creation and even Satan himself reinforcing the fight against us. And it is our fight. It is our task to fight with all we've got against the old man and the world and Satan. It is hard work.

Of course, we do not fight alone; we fight in the power of the Spirit. And in truth, it is Christ, our champion, who finally does all the fighting that needs to be done. And yet today, the Bible makes clear, we are still each charged to take up the fight ourselves. So fight we must. Luther knew this fight well and wrote often and forcefully about his warfare against the forces of evil arrayed against the new man he sought to be. He knew that a delightful, ringing, pure proclamation of the Gospel does not cancel or make irrelevant the call into pitched battle against sin and evil in the forms of our own flesh, the world, and the hordes of hell. Both realities—the fight already won by Christ and the fight ongoing in our daily existence—continue simultaneously as present and tangible experiences in the life of a Christian.

The Lutheran tradition has not always been as deliberate or adept as Luther at emphasizing both facets of the continuing reality of our Christian existence. The Gospel is too often arrayed against the ongoing battle as if fighting against sin somehow calls into question the power or reality of the Gospel. Much has been written about this false contrast, and the effort to reclaim a more prominent place within Lutheranism for the work of formation to the Christian life, the work of fighting against sin and evil, indeed for the work of discipleship, has made some headway. But while this effort has been mounted with a degree of vigor, there has been too little attention devoted to thoughtful Lutheran explorations of the actual content of such warfare against sin.

In other words, while there has been a fair amount of effort invested in arguing for the place of character formation, training in discipleship, and the pursuit of moral and pious behavior within a Lutheran theological framework, there has not been a great deal of work committed to spelling out, teaching, and encouraging the specifics of what it might look like to engage in the actual warfare against sin and the old man. Mike Fieberkorn has worked hard to fill this void.

I know that Mike has worked hard; he was my graduate student. But hard academic and doctrinal work was perhaps not the most significant part of the work that drove the present book into publication. Rev. Dr. Fieberkorn is first Pastor Fieberkorn. He serves a flock of real sheep. His love for his people and his striving to help those real people receive the Gospel and then learn to live like the Christians God declares them to be are perhaps the most significant factors shaping this book. On a weekly if not daily basis, a pastor sees the bitter reality of the battle against the old man and the damage inflicted by sin in the lives of Christian people. It is not intellectual theory, philosophical reflection, or doctrinal speculation that animates this book. It is the suffering of real people, the yearning of actual saints to live more faithfully and more fully in accord with God's plan, and the need for real people to have concrete guidance in their fight against their own sinful flesh, the world, and the devil that give this book a tone that is relevant, vibrant, and urgent.

To provide the specificity and applicability needed, Dr. Fieberkorn revives a rich and deeply rooted tradition within the church: the identification and consideration of the vices and the virtues. However, he does this from a Lutheran perspective. Given the commitments and proclivities of these distinct ecclesial traditions, it perhaps goes without saying that bringing them together is no small feat. But Mike has good counsel and guidance in the endeavor: Luther himself leads the way. The pages that follow tell the story of Martin Luther's role and the correlation of vice and virtue with the reformer's explicit teaching on the Decalogue. But more important, in the pages that follow you will find exactly the sort of concrete and specific direction, encouragement, and strategies you need for the very real fight that must define and propel your daily Christian walk.

Through the power of the Holy Spirit, perhaps this book will have the best result of all: one more life more closely aligned with the reality of redemption already fully accomplished by Christ.

Rev. Dr. Joel D. Biermann

Waldemar A. and June Schuetle Professor of Systematic Theology
Concordia Seminary, St. Louis

PREFACE

THE BATTLE IN EVERY BELIEVER'S SOUL

Many Christians mistakenly think that following Jesus will be relatively easy. Children complete confirmation instruction and feel as if a very large part of their work in the faith is now complete. A newly married husband and wife join a congregation and are baptized, expecting life to run more smoothly now that they are part of a church and worship regularly. Adult Christians who have been believers since the day they were baptized as infants assume they don't have to do anything, because they are saved by grace alone and Jesus has already done it all. We might get the impression that faith, once begun, can be set on cruise control until eventually we arrive at the intended destination.

Experience shows that little could be further from reality.

Far too often, confirmands quickly drop the habit of weekly worship once they enter high school, and by college many have abandoned the faith altogether. The newly Christian couple soon experiences some unexpected adversity in their lives, and then they are largely absent. Lifelong Christians repeatedly give in to sins they dismiss as minor while their faith erodes until at some point they admit they no longer really believe. Perhaps you have had moments when you felt as if your faith was starting to slip away.

Why does this happen?

In instances like these, we must recognize that many Christians are not prepared for the battle that ensues within every believer's soul following faith.

Jesus explains these different experiences in His parable about a man sowing the seeds of faith (Matthew 13:1–9, 18–23). A seed that lands on the hard path (a hardened heart) never takes root. It is not understood, and the devil snatches it up immediately. But other seeds fall into different kinds of soil and begin to grow. Seed that lands in rocky, shallow soil might shoot up quickly, but without deep roots, it is easily scorched when the troubles of life inevitably come. Seed that lands in thorny soil does well for a time until the thorns of worldly cares and deceitful riches eventually choke it out; in the end, it proves unfruitful.

Satan does not waste his time on those already in a state of unbelief. So if you do believe, you should expect to fight for your faith to endure over the long run. Roaring lion that he is, the devil persistently prowls around looking for another soul to devour, enticing you with the things of this world, seducing you to surrender to your own sinful desires, and hoping these repeated forays will ultimately obliterate your faith.

It's no surprise, then, that Paul exhorts young Timothy to "fight the good fight of the faith" (1 Timothy 6:12). Peter warns the entire church to "abstain from the passions of the flesh, which wage war against your soul" (1 Peter 2:11). The Bible teaches that a daily battle takes place inside the soul of everyone who believes. On one side stands the Holy Spirit, desiring to form us into the new people we have been made through Baptism. On the other side stand our sinful desires, the world, and the devil himself, and they fight vehemently against the work of the Spirit. As the Holy Spirit labors continually to renew us in the image of God, the allures of the world and the desires of the flesh distract us, and Satan wants to use them to do nothing less than destroy our souls.

Martin Luther tied this ongoing battle directly to Holy Baptism. In his Small Catechism, Luther first taught clearly about the benefits that Baptism gives: "It works forgiveness of sins, rescues from death and the devil, and gives eternal salvation to all who believe this, as the words and promises of God declare."[1] These simple words convey so much. In your own Baptism, your sins were washed away, you were promised that one day you would be raised with Christ and overcome death, and you were given the gift of faith and eternal salvation. All of this is possible because when you were baptized, you were snatched from Satan's kingdom and made God's child and an heir of His heavenly kingdom. Being baptized means you are saved without a doubt. It is certain assurance for the soul. But it also means that Satan is going to do everything in his power to get you back. The battle of the soul is now begun.

Luther went on to address this. As he concluded his discussion on Baptism, he finally asked,

> **What does such baptizing with water indicate? It indicates that the Old Adam in us should by** daily contrition and repentance **be drowned and die with all sins and evil desires, and** that a new man should daily emerge **and arise to live before God in righteousness and purity forever.**[2]

This is a picture of the daily war being waged within the soul. Here Luther taught us that the Christian must daily fight against the old Adam (that is, the sinful nature that dwells within each of us from conception) as part of the ongoing battle of faith. Simply put, if we do not repeatedly drown and put to death our sins and evil desires, the new man is never permitted to emerge. In time, even our trust in Jesus can be abandoned.

Luther treated the nature of this battle in more detail in his Large Catechism—with a twist. He described the daily battle of the baptized soul specifically in terms of the believer's movement from vice to virtue:

> A Christian life is nothing else than a daily baptism, begun once and continuing ever after. For we must keep at it without ceasing, always purging whatever pertains to the old Adam, so that whatever belongs to the new creature may come forth. What is the old creature? It is what is born in us from Adam, *irascible* [*angry*], *spiteful, envious, unchaste* [*lustful*], *greedy, lazy* [*slothful*], *proud*—yes—and unbelieving; it is beset with all *vices* and by nature has nothing good in it. Now, when we enter Christ's kingdom, this corruption must daily decrease so that the longer we live the more *gentle, patient*, and *meek* we become, and the more we break away from *greed, hatred, envy*, and *pride*. This is the right use of baptism among Christians, signified by baptizing with water. Where this does not take place, but rather the old creature is given free rein and continually grows stronger, baptism is not being used but resisted.[3]

As Luther showed, living out our Baptism entails not only the active slaying of various vices (things like anger, envy, and greed) but also the daily rising up of dispositions characteristic of the new man (virtuous qualities such as gentleness, patience, and meekness). When we neglect this task, we are choosing not to make use of our Baptism—even to resist it! In other words, those who have been baptized must engage each waking day in the battle of the soul. Failure to do so fights against the work the Spirit is trying to accomplish in and through us and even against the very promises that have been granted us in our Baptism! Luther consistently talked this way about how Baptism ought to shape our lives.

Now, about those vices Luther used to describe the sinful nature—that list happens to include six of the seven vices known as the seven deadly sins, a specific grouping of vices that has existed in the tradition of the church for over fourteen hundred years. Originally, these were called capital or chief vices, rather than "deadly sins," a term which came much later. They were considered source sins, the evil habits of the inner heart from which all other sins ultimately arise. The commonly recognized seven deadly sins are pride, envy, anger, sloth, greed, gluttony, and lust.

In the quotation above, Luther mentioned all but gluttony. He used this list as a time-honored way to depict the essence of what sin looks like in the life of a Christian. However, if you know much about Luther, you might be surprised that he would evoke the cultural memory of such a list. Luther often lamented how earlier theologians had used the vice and virtue tradition to obscure the clear truth of the Gospel. However, when it came to the task of engaging in the battle of the soul, Luther found the categories of vice and virtue to be most helpful, and he employed these terms frequently.

This book will show how Luther reformed our understanding of vice and virtue and was able to make use of a revered theological tradition, despite his antagonism toward its problematic aspects. The old understanding of vice and virtue had indeed undermined the Gospel. Luther had to reimagine the concepts of vice and virtue before using them in the context of sanctified living. Part 1 of this book tells how he did so, reenvisioning vice and virtue in light of the Reformation tenet of salvation by grace alone and making use of this enduring tradition in a manner consistent with the Gospel of our Lord Jesus Christ.

Luther's reforming of vice and virtue also enhances our understanding of what it means to daily live baptized. Part 2 of the book considers how various vices and virtues vie for control of our hearts in the battle that takes place in every Christian's soul. We will explore how practically to slay vice and cultivate virtue that we might increasingly be freed from the bondage of unholy habits and be enabled to turn our attention toward the needs of our neighbor.

I pray this book will serve as a helpful guide as readers endeavor to shun the desires of the flesh and walk according to the Spirit. Through Luther's reformed understanding of vice and virtue, I trust readers will not only grow in their understanding of Christian truth but also be strengthened in the fight of their own daily battle with sin, and that by learning how to better engage in this battle, they will be able more faithfully and consistently to live out God's holy commands in their lives, that God would be honored and the neighbor served in love.

> Beloved, I urge you as sojourners and exiles to
> abstain from the passions of the flesh, which wage
> war against your soul.
>
> (*1 Peter 2:11*)

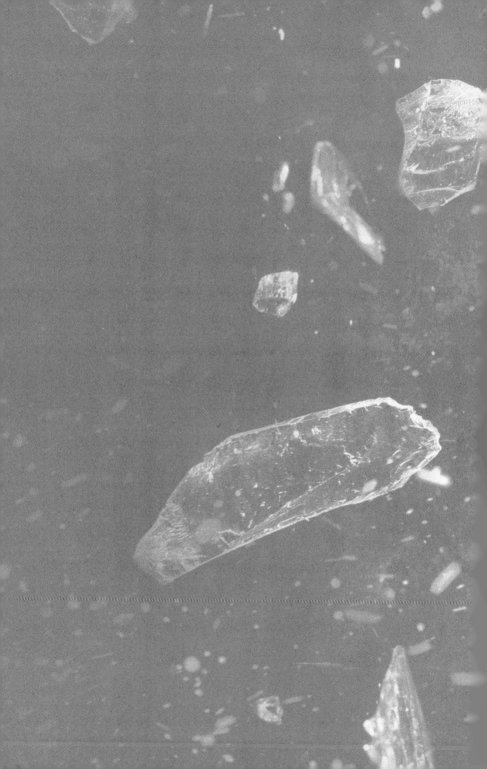

INTRODUCTION
VICE AND VIRTUE IN LUTHER

Salvation Not by Virtue

Even the most casual student of world history knows Martin Luther for his association with the Reformation of the Christian Church. The Reformation movement centered on the answer to this question: How are sinners saved from the wrath of a holy God?

Luther believed that the answer to that question favored by the church of his day was at odds with Scripture. Over time, the Roman Catholic Church had intermingled human performance into God's free gift of grace. This introduced doubt in the hearts and minds of the faithful about their salvation. If works were part of the equation, they would always wonder, Have I done enough? Have I done enough good works in my life that I might expect God to judge me favorably in the end and thus be saved from punishment in hell following my death?

Believers had begun to lose sight of the unconditional love of God shown in Christ Jesus. They saw God not as compassionate and forgiving but rather as an almighty, righteous judge. To be sure, God is both mighty and righteous, and He will return to judge the living and the dead on the Last Day—but on what basis? The Catholic Church of Luther's day might have answered, "On the basis of how well we have loved." In their minds, grace was like a spiritual power that God gives to humans to improve themselves; the grace was indeed given freely, but what use people might make of it was up to them! As such, much was made of moral progress, and one's relative performance with respect to the works of the Law were seen as part of the equation when calculating whether one would be saved. As a pious Christian shaped by the church of Rome, Luther grew up immersed in this concept of salvation.

But Luther eventually recognized the error of this understanding. Luther struggled to feel accepted by God and confident before the throne of judgment, continually tortured by the idea that God was angry with him. His outlook changed, though, as he studied Scripture. He began to see his God in a different light—as a God of love—as he read the New Testament, especially Paul's letters. Luther later recounted that famous moment while studying the letter to the Romans in the castle tower when he felt as if he had been "altogether born again and had entered paradise itself through open gates."[1]

He particularly recalled studying Romans 1:17, which speaks of the "righteousness of God [that] is revealed from faith." When Luther had read this verse before, he had always considered the phrase "the righteousness of God" to refer to the righteousness which *is* God's, with which He stands over us as our righteous judge. But through his study of Scripture, Luther came to realize that the "righteousness of God" Paul speaks of here was actually the righteousness we possess *from* God, bestowed on us through our faith in Jesus.

The more Luther studied, the more convinced he became that the biblical understanding of salvation was as Paul writes in numerous places: we are saved by faith alone, apart from the works of the Law (see Romans 3:28 and Galatians 2:16, for example). Grace is not a measurable quantity of power that God pours into us to be used by us; rather, grace is best conceived of as God's new attitude toward humanity because of the forgiving work of His Son. Because the sins of humanity have been atoned for in Christ, God now looks upon us with favor. In this understanding, we can know we are saved, not by considering whether we have done "enough," but by trusting the reality that, in Jesus, God has shown mercy to us and has already done it all on our behalf. In other words, salvation has nothing to do with me or my performance of good works—it has everything to do with Jesus and His work of dying on the cross for the sins of the world and being raised to life on the third day for our justification. We are justified by God's righteous declaration. He renders that verdict not because our moral performance substantiates our innocence but because the blood of Jesus covers our sin.

Undoing Aristotle

Once Luther believed he had arrived at a correct understanding of the Gospel, he began to teach the laity the true nature of salvation. He tirelessly reinforced these truths in the sermons he preached to his congregation, as he taught his students in the university classroom, and as he distributed his writings. To a people who had generally lived in fear of God's judgment, the pure Gospel of salvation by grace alone was good news indeed. But old habits die hard. To help the laity avoid returning to their old mindset, Luther also worked to dismantle parts of the distorted belief system of his day that had fostered an incorrect understanding of the Gospel.

In this respect, no system drew more of Luther's ire than the teachings of the philosopher Aristotle. Thomas Aquinas had adapted Aristotle's vice and virtue tradition for use in the church in the thirteenth century, and that practice shaped the church academics (known as the Scholastics) and the development of their own theological system. The Scholastics taught, among other things, that the inner desire to sin (called *concupiscence*) was not sinful in and of itself; sin occurred only when such desires were acted upon. They considered desires to be merely the "tinder of sin" that became sinful only when engulfed by the flames of evil deeds. The Scholastics also taught that the old sinful self had to be continually cleansed until one became perfectly holy. While it was theoretically possible for this process to be completed during one's earthly life, the common understanding was that some of the necessary cleansing would remain to be completed after one's death. This was the purpose of purgatory: to purge away the rest of the sinful self so the full blessings of salvation could commence. In their understanding, God would never declare righteous someone who was still very much a sinner. A favorable declaration from God could come only when all sin had been completely cleansed.

In contrast, Luther taught that Christians are simultaneously sinner and saint our entire lives. The old, sinful self that remains in every believer would be done away with completely at death and only the saint would remain. For Luther, the reality that we remain sinners did not negate God's declaration that we are entirely innocent of those sins during our earthly lives. Indeed, sinners cling to that promise in Christ for the assurance of salvation, even as we daily battle against the sinful nature.

Prior to Luther, one of the ways a Christian could gauge progression toward holiness was to avoid vices and embrace holy virtues. This concept of vice and virtue was synthesized into the theology of the church primarily by Thomas Aquinas, who appropriated it from the pagan ethicist Aristotle. In his famous writings on ethics, Aristotle systematically described what he observed to be primary virtues and their related vices of excess and deficiency. Virtues were good habits, and vices were the bad habits that resulted when someone practiced a virtue too much or too little. Take the virtue of generosity, for example. Consistently giving of your own possessions for the sake of others would make you virtuous. However, you could give too excessively, to the point where you would foolishly give away too much and neglect to provide for those under your care. This would be the vice Aristotle called liberality. On the other hand, you could refuse to give away anything at all, keeping the entirety of your money and goods for yourself. This, too, would be a vice, a deficiency in giving, often labeled miserliness, like Scrooge.

Aristotle did not consider vices sinful; rather, they were simply a weakness of character that people could overcome by the repeated practice of virtue as they slowly formed a new character. This understanding worked well as Thomas Aquinas adopted these concepts to teach about morality. The way to salvation could be viewed as using the grace God has granted to gradually overcome bad habits and become better and better people so that eventually we could be declared righteous and worthy of eternal life. The discerning reader can see how this framework hinders a biblical understanding of the Gospel—that we are saved by grace alone, not by our human performance. Because of this, Luther considered Aristotle's ethics to be "the worst enemy of grace" and worked to diminish its influence in the church.[2]

Reforming Vice and Virtue

And yet, if you read Luther's writings with an eye for the language of vice and virtue, there is more of this sentiment than you would expect. How was Luther able to use such terminology, given the threat Aristotle's philosophy had posed to the Gospel? This book will answer that question fully, but simply put, just as Luther had to teach clearly about the nature of salvation, so, too, he had to provide clarity about the concepts of vice and virtue for the church. Luther taught that vices are nothing less than specific manifestations of unbelief that remain in the human heart. Virtues are more than good habits. They are dispositions worked in and through us by the Holy Spirit—and not just so that we become better people but rather to enable us to more consistently carry out the good works that God prepared in advance for our service to others.

If, as Luther taught, vice is not just a bad habit but rather evidence of unbelief, then failure to fight against vice could eventually result in losing our faith, as Paul teaches in 1 Timothy 1:19. That is why elsewhere he admonishes us to "put to death" our evil desires (Colossians 3:5) and why Peter encourages us to make every effort to add virtue to our faith (2 Peter 1:5). They remembered Jesus' warning that vices related to the riches and cares of the world are like weeds that can choke out faith (Matthew 13:22) and how He exhorts us to continually watch ourselves that we might remain in faith until the day of His return (Luke 21:34).

Luther's reformed understanding of vice and virtue helps us strive each day to carefully guard and watch over our faith, exactly as Jesus teaches us to do. And the key to this transformation, this movement from vice to virtue, is for believers to actively live out our Baptism: to daily put to death the old man—those remnants of unbelief that continue to reside in the human heart—so that the new man the Spirit is creating can daily rise up in virtue, the dispositions that equip Christians to carry out God's commands.

This is the battle that plays out day by day in the souls of all who are baptized and believe.

I believe; help my unbelief!

(*Mark 9:24*)

PART 1

VICE AND VIRTUE REFORMED

And so you must not imagine that the Christian's life is a standing still and a state of rest. No, it is a passing over and a *progress from vices to virtue*. . . . And those who have not been *en route* you should not consider Christians either.

Martin Luther, *Lectures on Galatians*

Would you have guessed that quote is from Luther? He is not exactly known as a proponent of virtue ethics. But by casting the vice and virtue tradition in a new light—the light of the Gospel—Luther was able to make considerable use of it. And what about the final part of this utterance, that those who are not making progress from vice to virtue should not even be considered Christians? How could Luther say such a thing—especially given his commitment to salvation apart from human performance?

Luther could say this because he rightly recognized vices as evidence of unbelief in the human heart. As such, when we do not endeavor to move away from vice and toward virtue, we essentially embrace the various idols that rule our hearts and minds. Instead, Christians must strive to slay the idols and grow in the Spirit. Luther called this movement from vice to virtue the "task of all whom [God] causes to be baptized."¹ Part 1 will explore the theology behind this task.

Little children, keep yourselves from idols.

(1 John 5:21)

CHAPTER 1

SINFUL DESIRE

THE OLD MAN THAT JUST WON'T DROWN

Mere Desire?

Picture yourself standing in worship. You've exchanged greetings and sung with gusto the opening hymn, one of your favorites. Your pastor made the sign of the cross over the congregation as he spoke the words of the invocation, invoking the name into which we are baptized—the name of the Father and of the Son and of the Holy Spirit. Then, prior to speaking together the corporate confession of sins, he calls upon worshipers to silently examine their hearts.

But today those few silent seconds seem like an eternity. Shame creeps in as you realize that you continue to confess the same sins of thought, word, and deed week after week. You wonder, Can't I ever get any better? As a Christian living out my faith, *shouldn't* I be getting a bit better?

As you take inventory, you realize there has been progress: I've gotten better at not yelling at my kids when I get angry, you think. That only happened once this week, and that is an improvement. It used to be an everyday occurrence. And, you recall, not once did I slam a door or pound my fist or make an obscene gesture at another driver who obviously doesn't understand the rules of the road. This, too, is an improvement—it used to happen at least once or twice a week.

Then you drop your head. You recognize that even though these things happen less frequently, what has *not* changed are the angry thoughts that simmer beneath the surface. Just because you don't yell doesn't mean you aren't as mad as you always are at the kids when they disobey. Just because you've been gentler on the door you've refrained from slamming doesn't mean you aren't still hot under the collar. Just because you didn't gesture at the other driver doesn't mean you aren't seething with road rage on the inside. So you wonder, Have I *really* gotten any better?

A few weeks passed, but it kept bothering you, so you confided this problem to a Christian friend over lunch. He encouraged your so-called progress. He assured you that everyone gets mad; as long as it doesn't boil over into words or actions, it's nothing to worry about. You're not so sure. The words of the Confession liturgy keep ringing in your head: "We have sinned against You in *thought*, word, and deed."[1] My *church* seems to think these angry thoughts are sinful, you conclude. But why? Getting angry seems like a feeling that arises apart from our overt will. Should I be held accountable for something I have so little control over?

Humans have wrestled with that question since the fall of man—should we feel guilty for sins of the heart? Over the ages, the church has given different answers about whether "mere" desire is morally neutral. Much like the friend in the example above, the Scholastics and the church of Luther's day believed it was neutral. They taught that such desire was merely tinder that turned into sin only when acted upon. Luther himself wrestled with this answer. It turns out, getting the answer right was a key component that drove the Reformation.

Desire Itself as Sinful

Most people rightly associate the Reformation with new insights about the nature of justification—that is, understanding that we are saved by grace through faith in Christ alone. But Luther arrived at this understanding in tandem with his recognition of the radical nature of sin, which imprisons man in complete bondage to unrighteousness. Scripture tells us that since humanity's fall into sin, "every intention of the thoughts of [our] heart is only evil continually" (Genesis 6:5). Sinful desire is always with us. This inner desire (or concupiscence) expresses itself specifically, for instance, when we lust or covet. Luther came to realize that the lustful or envious thoughts that give rise to evil deeds are by no means neutral—they, too, are evil.

Luther arrived at this understanding through his study of Paul's letter to the Romans: "[Paul] clearly adduces the moral law in Romans 7[:7], 'I should not have known that concupiscence is sin, if the law had not said, "You shall not covet."'" Luther admits that this doesn't necessarily make sense to us:

> For nature did not call this wanton itching [that is, coveting] sin, but rather its evil use on the bodies of others, as in debauchery, adultery, and fornication. Similarly, it does not call anger and avarice sin, but rather their expression in theft, fraud, slander, murder—and so also for other vices.[2]

To our fallen human minds, it does not seem like a mere

thought, such as anger or avarice (the desire for money or possessions), would be considered sinful. Rather, it seems as if these desires would only be sinful when expressed in the world. Anger is just in the mind, but when acted out to the fullest extent, it could lead to murdering another. Similarly, a greedy thought might not seem overly problematic, but when it leads to someone stealing, then it appears sinful indeed.

But Paul clearly writes that God's command in Scripture not to covet (the Ninth and Tenth Commandments) shows us that even our covetous desires should be considered sinful. Opposing those who labeled desire as only weakness or imperfection, Luther boldly declared, "Here we stand at a parting of the ways. . . . I have Paul's term on my side."[3] Contrary to what we might suppose, these inner desires—that is, habitual vices like anger, greed, or lust—are sinful in and of themselves. God's Word calls us to acknowledge the reality that sin exists, not just at the level of the outward deed, but within the deepest desires of our fallen hearts.

Vices as Evidence of Original Sin

Luther's burgeoning understanding led him to recognize that the presence of these sinful desires is evidence that original sin remains in our hearts even after we come to faith. He writes:

> The last two commandments are perfectly clear. They forbid sinful lusts of the flesh and the coveting of temporal goods. These evil desires do no harm to our neighbor, and yet they persist to the

grave. . . . Nobody has ever been so holy that he never felt some evil inclination within. . . . For original sin is born in us by nature: it may be checked, but it cannot be entirely uprooted except through death.[4]

While the Scholastics taught that desires were mere defects or weaknesses, Luther found from Scripture that this was not true. Indeed, he noted that "it is contrary to Scripture, for St. Paul does not say, 'I find in me a defect,' but expressly . . . 'The *sin* which dwells within me' [Romans 7:20]." Luther also pointed out that when Paul "writes to baptized people . . . 'The desires of the flesh are against the spirit, and the desires of the spirit are against the flesh' [Galatians 5:17]," Paul teaches that these desires come from our "physical birth, when this original sin of evil desire is born with them." Luther then explained that "this original sin, born in the flesh, passes away in baptism as guilt, but remains as work; although it is forgiven, nevertheless it lives, twists, turns, raves, and assails us."[5]

Here Luther carefully articulates how it can be taught that Baptism removes original sin and yet, when we experience sinful desire in our lives, it can still rightfully be attributed to our original sin. Baptism removes the *consequences* of original sin—in other words, the baptized will no longer be damned because of our sinful nature. And yet, the removal of this consequence does not mean the evil desires that emanate from original sin no longer exist. No, they are present, and the evidence for it is the vices that continue to exercise their hold on us: desires such as lust, anger, and greed. Theologian Karl Barth described this well (though the quote is often misattributed to Luther) when he said that though the old Adam within us was drowned in the waters of Holy Baptism, the fact remains that he is a very good swimmer![6] As long as we remain in this sinful flesh, it is impossible to completely drown the old, sinful man within us.

Luther was not the first to have this understanding. Augustine, one of Luther's greatest influences, had written on this subject in the fifth century. As Luther read Augustine's writings on the matter, he found consistency with Scripture and with his own position. Luther was fond of citing Augustine, saying that "all sin is forgiven in baptism, not so that it no longer exists, but so that it is no longer imputed."[7]

In light of the clear witness of Scripture, Luther became frustrated with the Scholastics for not recognizing the error of their ways. He chided the church's position:

> **While they write and say that evil desire in the Ninth and Tenth Commandments is no sin, they pretend at the same time to preach and teach both commandments, although in fact they permit evil desire and thus break the commandment of God.**

How could a Christian affirm the commandments that prohibit coveting while at the same time declare that inner desires that are contrary to God's will are no sin? This would mean one could have evil, covetous desire and yet remain righteous in God's sight. According to Luther, holding such a position makes both Moses and God out to be liars![8]

Luther took a hard look at all the commandments to illustrate how they apply not just to outward deeds but also to the inner motives of the sinful heart. For example, the church purported to hold the Sixth Commandment (forbidding adultery) in high esteem, but Luther pointed out that their willingness to turn a blind eye to rampant unchastity showed they did not take this commandment seriously. Similarly, the church cried loudly that one should not kill, but by teaching that one could be angry with one's enemy and remain without sin, they clearly had departed from the plain teaching of Scripture. Luther lamented how the church had obscured the reality of inner sin, allowing men to remain in inner vices such as envy and hatred, which he knew were prohibited by the same commandments that forbid outward deeds. This false understanding served to tear apart the true meaning of God's commands, ruining and misleading the people—causing them to sin inwardly in ways that Luther felt could be considered more harmful to the soul than some outward transgressions.[9]

What Vice Really Is

Thus, Luther's first step in reforming the church's understanding of vice is to show that inner desires are no neutral thing. He discerned that this false notion stemmed from Aristotle, who spoke of "affections which are in us but bring neither blame nor praise," much like the Scholastic idea of neutral desire. But Luther called Christians to turn from that unbiblical idea and "examine original sin diligently, to see what it is."[10]

As Luther explored "what sin really is," he came to a new conception of vice. This "new" conception placed him on par with the more ancient understanding of the vice tradition, which existed long prior to Scholasticism. Originally, those who had cataloged a list of capital vices saw them not as inert precursors to sin but rather as dangerous in and of themselves. Those vices were considered the origin of all sins, which, when allowed to run rampant, could lead to the loss of faith and the subsequent death of our souls—hence the eventual moniker of "deadly sins."

For these earlier theologians such as Augustine, for Luther, and most important, per Scripture, something such as a lustful thought is not a mere affection that becomes either a vice or virtue or tinder that becomes sinful only when enflamed by action. No, these thoughts are the essence of our sinful nature within— what Luther called the "motions of original sin" that reside in our members, wage war with our minds, and take us captive (Romans 7:23). Luther learned what sinful desire really is: not a defect in character, not a bad habit, and certainly not neutral, but something in us that "moves man to avarice, disobedience, and other vices."[11]

REFLECTION QUESTIONS

1. Read Genesis 6:5. How does this verse describe the nature of human beings after the fall into sin? How does this help us correctly assess our inner desires?

2. Read the Ten Commandments in Exodus 20:3–17 or Deuteronomy 5:7–21. Which commandments forbid outward actions? Which forbid inner sins of the heart?

3. Consider a sinful thought that you often struggle with. How does repeated engagement in sinful thinking turn into a habitual vice that becomes our normal way of looking at the world? How might this affect who we are becoming as God's people? How might it affect our neighbors?

4. Read Galatians 5:16–17. What do we learn about our desires in this passage? What kinds of things do sinful desires keep us from being able to do?

5. Read 1 Corinthians 10:12–13. According to this passage, are we powerless against the desires that rise up in our hearts and minds? What is the danger in ignoring or being unalarmed by temptation? What could it ultimately lead to?

6. Luther quipped, "You cannot prevent the birds from flying over your head, but you can certainly keep them from building a nest in your hair" (LW 42:73). How does this analogy reflect the relationship between sinful desire, vices, and outward manifestations of sin in our lives?

CHAPTER 2

A SIN BY
ANY OTHER
NAME

Fear, Love, and Trust

I've taught confirmation classes using Luther's Small Catechism for a number of years. A typical year begins with a presentation of the Ten Commandments and their meanings. For their memory work, kids are required to learn Luther's meaning of each commandment by heart. For some students, this is not difficult. For others, it's a struggle. By the fourth or fifth week, some students struggle to keep it all in their heads. But it seems everyone who has been through Lutheran confirmation remembers the meaning of the First Commandment (perhaps because it's the shortest!). I've met ninety-year-olds in the nursing home who still know it. I've met lapsed Lutherans who haven't been in church since confirmation, and even they can still usually remember: "You shall have no other gods. *What does this mean?* We should fear, love, and trust in God above all things."

As Christians, we are called to fear, love, and trust in God above everything else. Sounds pretty simple, doesn't it? Perhaps at first glance. But when we keep in mind Luther's insights from the previous chapter and acknowledge that original sin continually gives rise to evil desires within us, we quickly recognize the vast challenge this task poses for fallen human beings.

Exposing our inner desires as sinful was only the first phase in Luther's rehabilitation of our understanding of vice. Next we'll explore what leads us to embrace the unholy habits that rule our hearts and minds. Luther discerned that fear often causes us to take those first steps down the paths that lead to our darkest desires, and unless we look for help in the right place, that journey will always end in unbelief.

Fear in a Fallen World

Because we live in a broken world, we constantly face adversity and hardship in our lives. It can be frightening not knowing how we'll get through tough times. When we encounter these difficulties apart from faith in God's goodness, we grasp at something—anything—in our world to assuage these fears and give us a measure of peace.

Luther laments how desperate people are far too ready to "make a deal with the devil, in order that he may give them plenty of money, or help them in love affairs, preserve their cattle, restore to them lost possessions, and so forth" and how they "look to [God] for nothing good, nor do they seek good from Him."[1] The old man living inside each of us by nature does not trust God in our time of need but is always looking for help in other places.

Luther observed how people who do not trust in God then tend to become covetous or anxious. They place their hope in something like money or possessions, hoping these things will provide the comfort and security they seek. This not only impedes their ability to be generous toward others[2] but more tragically overlooks the one place where real help can be found—in the one true God. Luther recognized that to covet is to seek help in something other than the God who has promised to provide for all our needs of body and soul.

Love in All the Wrong Places

The things of the world often seem to provide the comfort we are looking for, which is why we can so easily be deceived by them.

Attempting to secure our future by building great wealth through a shrewd investment portfolio, for instance, provides a measure of solace against the unknown of tomorrow. And that consolation can persist for a long time—in some cases, even a lifetime. But the security we find in money is false. The possibility always remains that the wealth you have carefully built could come tumbling down in an instant with the next stock market crash. Then the security you thought you possessed is exposed for the ruse it is.

More often, though, we are enticed because worldly solutions appear more powerful and seem to promise more immediate results than God, who sometimes seems distant or, at least, not interested in helping us. Because of this perception, the things of this world have a powerful ability to elicit our love. Luther spells out the predictable pattern sinners fall into in their time of need: "First one overlooks the Creator, takes pleasure in the creature, and clings to it as though it were good. . . . Next the habit of loving it is established, and thus, the heart is hardened toward . . . the Creator."[3] When we look to the world for comfort and the things of the world seem to meet our present need, we begin to love those things more than we love our God.

In fact, this is how Thomas Aquinas and the Scholastic tradition typically spoke of sin—it was simply a matter of disordered love. It isn't wrong to love money, they reasoned, so long as you don't love it more than you love God or your neighbor. They taught that the key to overcoming sin and vice was to prioritize the things you love in the right order. Dante's classic work *The Divine Comedy*, written less than a century after Aquinas lived, demonstrates how prominently the Scholastic concept of sin was embedded in the minds of the faithful. The poem's subsequent popularity and enduring appeal further reinforced that understanding.

Purgatorio, the second part of Dante's poem, follows travelers as they are cleansed of various sins on their journey up a mountain toward Paradise. The poem is organized according to the seven deadly vices, beginning at the bottom with pride and continuing upward with envy, anger, sloth, greed, gluttony, and finally lust. As he narrates his tale, Dante characterizes the vices as disordered love.[4] Pride, envy, and anger are examples of perverted love, occurring when people pursue otherwise worthy goals in a misguided manner. Sloth is an example of insufficient love, a vice that occurs when we are indifferent about the needs of our neighbor. The last three vices—greed, gluttony, and lust—are examples of excessive love, those times when human beings love the things of this world more than they should.

There is a degree of truth behind this analysis of our desires. Vices are indeed evidence that our priorities in life have become jumbled, and we'll explore this concept more in the second half of the book. But Luther recognized this is only part of the story. He knew that to love created things more than our Creator is an indication of an even deeper issue: man's prideful attempt to secure his own destiny apart from God's help.

The Problem of Pride

It became increasingly clear to Luther that all sin, however characterized, was rooted in a prideful heart whereby we put our trust in the wrong places—or the wrong person: "Those who do not trust in God at all times and do not see God's favor and grace and good will toward them . . . seek his favor in other things *or even in themselves.*" Man's problem is not only trusting in worldly things, but pridefully trusting in himself over and above God. Once again, Augustine and other ancient church fathers helped Luther arrive at this understanding: "In all of these [sinful] deeds we can see the same thing: *love of self* which seeks its own advantage, robs both God and one's neighbor of their due, and concedes neither to God nor any man anything they have, or are, or could do or become. Augustine expressed this succinctly when he said, 'Self-love is the beginning of every sin.'"[5]

Luther drew from Augustine and other early church fathers to recover something that the Scholastics had lost sight of: the overarching problem of pride that lurks behind every vice. Consider the nature of anger. When we are angry at others, what is really going on in our hearts? We witness an injustice, and we want those in the wrong to be punished. But we are afraid they won't be. So we wrest justice out of God's hands and pridefully decide we are better judges than He is. Our attempt to mete out vengeance In His stead is then expressed in anger. This is just one example of how our every vice is, at root, a prideful attempt to do for ourselves those things that are rightly reserved for God to accomplish.▼

▼ Luther also acknowledged how avarice (or more commonly, greed) sometimes competes with pride for status as the ultimate source sin that gives rise to all others. In his late Genesis lectures, for instance, he affirmed: "Avarice and pride at the core are the root of all evils" (LW 8:63). Here Luther takes his cue from Scripture, specifically Paul in 1 Timothy 6:10 ("the love of money is the root of all kinds of evil"), and so he is also able to refer to avarice as "the home and training ground of all vices" (LW 6:7).

But Luther took his own analysis of sin one step further. Yes, he acknowledged, vices result from fear, which compels our sinful nature to grasp at the things of this world to find comfort and subsequently to love those things in a disordered manner. And yes, Luther granted, our love of self results in a prideful disposition that causes us to trust in ourselves more than God. But ultimately, Luther recognized what others in his day seemingly would not: that to usurp God's role and to trust in other things or oneself is nothing other than idolatry. As he wrote in the Large Catechism, "Confidence and faith of the heart alone make both God and an idol. . . . Whatever you set your heart on and put your trust in is truly your god."[6]

The covetous desires of our fallen hearts that seek the comfort of God in other places are simply ways idols rule our hearts and minds. Again, Luther's teaching had clear support in Scripture. He wrote: "The Apostle [Paul] calls no other sin idolatry except covetousness [Ephesians 5:5; Colossians 3:5], because this sin shows most starkly that man does not trust God for anything, but expects more benefit from his money than from God." Later he again expressed this sentiment, but used another term to describe the reality of our idolatry, this time labeling our proclivity to covet "the fruit of pernicious unbelief."[7]

If idolatry is trusting in something other than the true God, then it must be recognized that this misplaced trust is spurred by our disbelief that God is good and wants to help us. In other words, idolatry is unbelief. Here, at last, we see why vices pose such grave danger to our souls. While the first step in Luther's reformed understanding of the vices was simply to demonstrate that they are indeed sinful, the second step was his recognition that they are nothing less than idols—idols that are present due to our lack of trust in God, idols that are evidence of unbelief in our hearts, idols that, if allowed to rule our hearts, could result in the loss of faith altogether.▾

Let's allow Luther to complete his line of thinking from earlier in the chapter:

> **First, one overlooks the Creator, takes pleasure in**
> **the creature, and clings to it as though it were good.**
> **... Next, a habit of loving it is established, and thus**
> **the heart is hardened toward ... the Creator. ...**
> *Then unbelief follows.*

When it comes to vices, Luther concluded that "God has rightly included all things, not under anger or lust, but under unbelief." Simply put, "Unbelief is every vice."[8]

Every Sin an Idol

For Luther, all specific sins, however they might be labeled or described, were but symptoms of idolatrously clinging to false

---

▾ The table "Vices as Manifestations of Unbelief" at the back of this book illustrates this progression. It summarizes how every vice is related to aspects of our fear, love, and trust in God and how Luther moved beyond the tradition that preceded him to expose vices as specific manifestations of unbelief that arise in the human heart. This table also provides a summary of the nature of each vice, which will be a helpful reference when reading part 2 of this book.

gods. This view quickly became the way he taught others to comprehend sin. In a sermon he preached on the First Commandment, Luther explained:

> One who fears something else and trusts it makes of it a god. . . . You see, then, what faith is and what idolatry is. If you fear the prince more than God, then the prince is your god. If you trust your wife or money more than God, then these are your god. But God is held not in the hand but in the heart. If you fear him and trust him then you need fear no one and trust no one except God. Therefore the first commandment claims the two parts of your heart: fear God and trust him.[9]

The only person we should fear is God. The person we should love above all else is God. The only person in whom we should place our trust is God. Stated more succinctly, "We should fear, love, and trust in God above all things"—just as we learn in confirmation class. Failure to do so carries over and is involved in the breaking of all God's Commandments. Luther made this connection when he penned the meanings for the rest of the Ten Commandments in the Small Catechism. After the First Commandment, each commandment's meaning begins with the same words: "We should fear and love God so that . . ." By using the same language he used to explain the First Commandment, Luther tied the breaking of every other commandment to the breaking of the First.

In other words, if we could keep the First Commandment and avoid idolatry, we would easily be able to observe all the other commandments. After all, if we completely trusted God to provide for our needs, who would feel the need to steal? If we completely trusted God to watch over our reputation, who would be compelled to bear false witness? But because we are all by nature idolaters, we break every other command. The breaking of any commandment is but a symptom of the real problem at work: a failure to fear, love, and trust in God. If I disobey the authorities in my life and break the Fourth Commandment, the cause of this sin is my lack of trust that the authorities God has placed over me as His representatives are adequate. I attempt to act in God's stead by defying them and becoming an authority unto myself. The named sin may be disobedience, but the underlying sin, at its base, is nothing other than idolatrous pride.

Here's what Luther knew: We can reason about how our fears give impetus to exercise our sinful desires. We can recognize when our love for something in the world is given too high a priority in our lives. We can even discern how the prideful love of self is behind every misdeed. But this truth remains—a sin by any other name is still an idol.

REFLECTION QUESTIONS

1. Read the lists of sins in Colossians 3:5; Galatians 5:19–21; and 1 Peter 4:3. How do each of these sins amount to idolatry, that is, trusting in something other than God?

2. Read 1 John 2:16. Name some sins that belong in each of the worldly categories listed: lust of the eyes, lust of the flesh, and the pride of life. Which category do you struggle with most?

3. Read 1 John 5:21 and 1 Corinthians 10:14. What do John and Paul tell us to do any time we encounter idolatry? How can you do this in your life?

CHAPTER 3

VICES

THE UGLY FACES
OF UNBELIEF

What's Your Favorite Ugly Face?

In 1977, a struggling musician from Levittown, New York, was at a crossroads. He had released four albums and a couple of minor hits, but if not for the success of his next album, his days as a singer-songwriter might have been over. Instead, he would eventually put out thirteen studio albums over a twenty-year recording career, all enabled by the one that propelled him to fame. The album's first single, "Just the Way You Are," would go on to win Grammys for record and song of the year.[1] Billy Joel's album *The Stranger* has now sold over eleven million copies. You might even be able to sing along with some of its songs: "Only the Good Die Young," "Vienna," "Movin' Out," "She's Always a Woman," and "Scenes from an Italian Restaurant" all remain largely recognizable and enjoy regular airplay, decades after they were released.

But I'd like you to consider the theme of the title track. In "The Stranger," Joel sings about the strange "faces" we eventually see in our significant other. We may have thought we really knew the person we fell in love with, that there was nothing we had not seen, but then, Joel says, one day a "stranger" appears in the face we thought we knew. Joel's lyrics point out the reality that we all have these faces—strange faces we keep hidden but eventually put on when we give in to our desires.

I don't know for certain what kinds of faces Joel meant, but perhaps he had in mind some character flaw (some vice!) in your partner that takes you completely by surprise. We all have these faces, Joel insists, and the truth is we enjoy trying them on. Our vices allure us, promising a shortcut to happiness, success, and the good life. Who doesn't momentarily feel better after lashing out in anger at an injustice or after binge eating to waylay some stress? That's why we love them so much—for the quick fix they at first glance seem to provide.

But these are empty promises. These sinful habits can give only the temporary illusion of comfort. In the end, every vice will fail us, as any idol ultimately will; only God can provide true identity, security, and meaning in our lives. Still, because we are accustomed to chasing after these counterfeit gods and the fleeting relief they provide, they can come to dominate our lives and cause us to act in ways that surprise even ourselves. It gets so easy to continually put them on. It takes intentional effort to replace these destructive habits with the holy habits of Christian living.

So what's your favorite ugly face to put on? Maybe it's the face of anger you put on for your husband the other day, a face that appeared strange indeed for a woman he'd never before seen so upset. Maybe it's the lazy face you put on for your wife. When you were dating, you always offered to help with chores, but now you are content to watch football while she does endless loads of laundry alone. Maybe it's the envious face you put on when you hang out with your friends—you're always talking about others behind their backs, pining away and wishing you had their lives instead of your own. Whatever it is, you are not alone. The faces humans wear at their worst are prevalent, predictable, and all too recognizable. And any ugly face we might show has particular characteristics and a particular name.

Vices, it turns out, do a very good job naming our ugly sides. Since vices are ways unbelief crops up in our lives, naming them helps us accurately diagnose how we might be developing a tendency to trust something in this world more than the true God. When you examine your own life, what vices do you see? Do you have the courage to name yours?

The Vice Tradition

We could say that the tradition of labeling sins through vices started with Jesus Himself! Consider when Jesus taught the disciples about the source of sin:

> **For from within, *out of the heart of man*, come evil thoughts, sexual immorality, theft, murder, adultery, coveting, wickedness, deceit, sensuality, envy, slander, pride, foolishness. All these evil things come *from within*, and they defile a person.** (Mark 7:21–23, emphasis added)

The source of all sin is the fallen heart, a heart that due to original sin desires evil things. Out of this sinful heart arises any and every sin that could be named. Jesus lists some outward sins, such as theft, murder, adultery, and slander. But He also names inner sins—the "evil thoughts" that begin the list, the sins that no one might know about except the sinner himself. In time, the church would label these kinds of sins "vices," and Jesus includes several here: coveting, envy, pride. Likewise, the apostle Paul wrote various sin lists in his letters (such as 1 Corinthians 6:9–10; Galatians

5:19–21; and Colossians 3:5–8, to name a few). Those lists, too, identify both the outward sins enacted against our neighbors and the sins beneath the surface, simmering in the heart until they bubble up into some visible manifestation for all to see.

One early Christian monk picked up on the reality of these evil thoughts and developed a theology to categorize those inner desires. Evagrius of Pontus, from the late fourth century, lived the last period of his life in isolation in North Africa, having fled from his prior positions within the church because of his own sinful struggles. He served as a lector under Basil the Great and later as a deacon under Gregory of Nazianzus, during which time he became aware of pride welling up in his heart because of his skill as an orator. Then, when he found himself lusting after another man's wife, an infatuation he could not seem to shake, he became alarmed for his spiritual well-being and attempted to escape temptation in the solitary cloister of the monastery. But isolation did not stop his base desires. Through his continued battle with sin, Evagrius found that eight sinful thoughts were always with him, and he developed a concept of vices from which all other sins arise: pride, vainglory, anger, sloth, sadness, greed, gluttony, and lust.[2]

Other influential Christians adapted his concepts, including St. Benedict and eventually Pope Gregory the Great in the sixth century. Gregory adjusted the list based on his own reflections on vice. First, he noticed that several of the vices were similar, eventually combining first vainglory with pride and then sadness with sloth. Second, Gregory added another vice his experience had shown him was incredibly prevalent: envy. With that, the list came to seven vices, and it has remained intact ever since. Early on, they were called the "capital vices," recognizing how as base desires they serve as the origin of every other sin. But when these vices become habits, they quickly steer us down the path that leads to spiritual death, so somewhere along the line they earned the title "deadly sins," and the name has stuck ever since.

Of course, there is nothing especially necessary about this exact list of seven, and some note that the seven deadly sins are not a specifically biblical list in that they do not occur in Scripture all together. However, all the vices are certainly present in Scripture, and this grouping has endured for centuries because of how useful it is for theological reflection on sin. One could perhaps think of an eighth or even a ninth evil inner desire that gives rise to other sin, but the list as it stands is a comprehensive diagnostic of the inner life of sin.

Luther Appropriates the Vice Tradition

Luther worked diligently to expose covetous desire as sinful and to show how every instance of sin is rightly characterized as idolatry and unbelief. But Luther also understood that sin is never generic; it always manifests itself particularly. In other words, sin does not exist in and of itself. It's an abstract concept, a category we use to label thoughts, words, and actions that are contrary to God's will. Whatever we are calling sinful is always some concrete instance of sin. For example, the unholy thought that rises from a wayward glance at an attractive person—that is indeed sinful, but *which* sin? Specifically, that's lust. The natural result of idolatry is always some particular vice that can be named. Luther consistently demonstrated his awareness of the deadly specificity and particularity of sin. In his early work on Romans, he noted how men are prone to "fashion a gracious God for themselves" and "worship the figment of their imagination more truly than the true God" and concluded that such "idolatry leads to a whirlpool of vices." Two decades later, he wrote that "unbelief brings with it all the other sins."[3]

Throughout his writing career, Luther made use of the traditional vice categories to call out specific manifestations of idolatry. In his 1515 lectures on the Psalms, for example, Luther discussed the reasons why some are "far away" from God and determined that their separation has been caused "by pride, greed, sloth, luxury [i.e., lust, from the Latin *luxuria* in Gregory's list], gluttony, anger, envy." In 1528, while lecturing on 1 Timothy, Luther commented: "In any kind of people I find Satan and the seven deadly sins." Another pertinent reference occurred in 1545, as Luther's life drew near its close. Reflecting on the life of Old Testament Joseph and considering his opponents in positions of power, Luther reasoned that "the seven deadly sins hold sway to a far greater extent [in the courts of men] than they do in the households of private persons."[4] These examples spanning the latter half of his life show how, rather than shun the categories of vice in favor of generic talk of sin, Luther used the vices as lively categories to illustrate the manifestation of sin—how it always appears in specific and sadly recognizable ways when it rears its ugly head in the lives of the faithful.

Because of these convictions, Luther generally refrained from discussing sin in generic terms. In fact, when writing against one of his early theological opponents, Luther argued one should use "unmistakable terms, not simply speaking of sin, but calling it by its names: anger, passion, covetousness." Such names, "by universal consent and in all languages, are customarily used to designate faults and sins," Luther pointed out. We see this emphasis on the explicit naming of sins in Luther's 1539 *On the Councils and the Church*: "We should be happy if there were no pride, avarice, usury, envy, drunkenness, gluttony, adultery, or wantonness among our people. But there is so much weakness and imperfection among us that we induce but a few to do these good works."[5]

Similarly, in the Large Catechism, Luther used vice language to vividly express the temptations humans face:

The old Adam . . . exerts himself and encourages us daily to unchastity, laziness, gluttony and drunkenness, greed and deception, to defraud our neighbor and to overcharge him. In short, the old Adam encourages us to have all kinds of evil lusts, which cling to us by nature and to which we are moved by the society. . . . [The world] drives us to anger and impatience . . . [so that] there is nothing but hatred and envy, hostility, violence and wrong, unfaithfulness, vengeance, cursing, railing, slander, pride and haughtiness, with useless finery, honor, fame, and power.[6]

While these vice lists go well beyond the traditional seven capital vices, they illustrate Luther's penchant for forthrightly and routinely addressing sin in all its terrible particularity.

Even in Luther's commentaries on Scripture, the categories of vice are never far away. In commentary on Psalm 45, Luther lamented "what a great disgrace it is that man's will should be turned from God, that he . . . is full of lust, pride, avarice, and the like"—clear examples of the capital vice categories. In commentary on the book of Romans, he pointed out that successfully enduring the temptations of vice strengthens us in their opposites:

> Thus luxurious living makes the soul more chaste when it attacks, pride makes the soul humbler, laziness makes it more active, avarice makes it more generous, anger, more mild, gluttony, more abstemious.[7]

Here, he included six of the seven capital vices and paired them with their corresponding virtues, early evidence that he saw virtuous living as the remedy to the specific vices that have us in their grip—a theme we will explore later.

The language of vice was one of the primary ways Luther described and distinguished the various sins of the inner heart that plague us all. Luther recognized that, when it comes to vices, the Christian has no escape. Every believer will struggle with at least one vice, if not more, at any given point in life. As Luther considered the true nature of sin, he taught:

It is indeed true that there is no one passion cease-
lessly driving us to distraction. Anger does not
always burn, evil desire does not always rage, we
are not constantly tormented with envy, but one of
these succeeds the other. When they all sleep, then
languor and sloth do not sleep. If you are strenu-
ously active, then pride awakens.[8]

When we think we've made headway against one of our sinful
habits, another is all too eager to take its place. We are all too
ready to don our ugly faces. However, the Holy Spirit, by means of
Word and Sacrament, works diligently to bring forth holy dispositions in the lives of baptized believers. As these virtuous habits
well up, their presence leaves less room in our hearts for sin and
vice. They take more control of our thoughts, words, and actions.
And rather than ugly vice, our faces begin to reflect something
new: the characteristics that the Holy Spirit is growing in the new
hearts we have been given in Christ.

REFLECTION QUESTIONS

1. Read Mark 7:14–23. What does Jesus teach about the source of all sin? What kind of things come from within our unclean hearts?

2. The New Testament includes various "sin lists." Pick a few of the following passages to read: Romans 1:26–31; 1 Corinthians 6:9–10; Galatians 5:19–21; Ephesians 4:25–31; Colossians 3:5–8; 2 Timothy 3:1–7. Which sins do these lists include? Which sins are mentioned multiple times? How does considering the "sin lists" in Scripture help us understand what sin looks like?

3. Try dividing the sins from those lists into two categories: outward deed and inner heart. Which sins occur in the heart? How does this help us diagnose the origin of our own struggles?

4. What is the biggest problem with sins of the inner heart? If no one else knows about them, what's the big deal?

CHAPTER 4

VIRTUES

THE NEW MAN
DAILY RISING

What Good Is Virtue?

Have you ever wondered what the ideal Christian would look like? How would they think, speak, and behave? What kind of qualities would they exemplify in their lives? Perhaps you are thinking of a shortcut answer: they would look like Jesus! And yes, it's true—as the only perfectly holy human, Jesus exemplifies perfect Christian behavior on earth. But what was *His* life marked by? What qualities did He exhibit as He lived? We can, after all, observe and seek to emulate the same qualities that animated His own life—in fact, these are the very qualities the Holy Spirit desires to continually grow within us.

Paul's list of the fruit of the Spirit in Galatians 5:22–23 details the qualities Christians will display in their lives. Joy, peace, patience, kindness—these dispositions are the hallmarks of Christians living in accordance with God's will. But none of these things are possible without first having faith in Jesus. When our lives reflect these dispositions, Christians acknowledge that they are gifts supplied by God Himself, not our own doing. Yet we are also called to actively cultivate this fruit in our hearts, as the rest of Galatians 5 shows, where Paul says we must "keep in step with the Spirit" (v. 25). Through careful study of the Scriptures, Luther came to this biblical understanding and reframed how Christians should understand virtue.

One understanding of virtue is that it helps humans improve as individuals. Aristotle, for example, taught that habitually performing virtuous actions would make one a more virtuous person.

Some theologians in Luther's day taught that virtuous actions would help humans obtain God's favor, that man must take the initiative and "do what is in him" to begin the path that leads toward perfection and eventually salvation. But as Luther had learned, fallen human nature is always with us, and that affects even our "virtuous" acts. No one can be made righteous by doing righteous things—only God can make us truly righteous. If we refrain from killing or committing adultery or even becoming angry, without God's grace, we still sin incessantly, because there is no escape from sinful desire. Luther recognized that even the greatest examples of Christian virtue, such as church fathers like Gregory and Benedict, could never rid themselves of every fleshly desire.[1]

On the surface, an individual's virtuous qualities might appear good and right, but without faith in God, "the devil rules even in the best virtues." Without faith, all virtues are merely show and make us the worst hypocrites. These works might "glitter very nicely" on the outside, Luther wrote, "but inwardly they remain full of malice, anger, hatred, pride, impatience, unchastity, etc.," because of our sinful nature. At the end of the day, even "the highest and most beautiful virtues . . . contribute nothing toward righteousness."[2]

This begs the question, "What does virtue profit if sins remain?"[3] Did Luther think virtue pointless? Hardly! While Luther firmly taught that virtuous works contribute nothing to our standing before God, he understood them to be quite valuable when it comes to keeping God's commands and serving our neighbor in Christian love.

Faith Comes First

For Luther, the key to any true concept of virtue was faith. Because the old Adam continues to live within us, faith must be present for any action to be truly virtuous, for "without faith . . . no work is a genuine living work." Thus, Luther could say, "faith in Christ is every virtue."[4] Just as idolatry was the common ingredient in every vice, so faith must be present in every good work.

Once faith is in place—that is, once we trust in the work of Jesus Christ on our behalf—various good works will flow from this virtue because faith is "the very first, highest, and best [work] from which all others must proceed, in which they must exist and abide." In other words, the faith we receive from God is always the starting point and source of Christian virtue. In particular, Luther recognized that love inevitably flows from this faith, and he therefore also described love as the "highest virtue."[5]

But Luther knew that, like sin, love is not a generic concept. Just as sin must be identified by its specific names, so love must be described specifically, so that it can be better understood and hence embraced by believers who endeavor to express their "faith working through love" (Galatians 5:6). While idolatry proliferates into various specific vices, faith and love manifest in "a multitude of the most beautiful virtues. . . . Faith is the mother, so to speak, from whom that crop of virtues springs."[6]

True Christian Virtue

But what are these particular virtues? In the philosophical tradition, the four cardinal virtues are prudence, justice, courage, and temperance. While Luther did occasionally acknowledge the value these civic virtues hold for society, he did not favor them to describe the distinctively Christian process of sanctification. The philosophical virtues, while they accord with natural law, do not always readily have their logical end in the neighbor—an important component of how Scripture depicts manifestations of love. We might expect that Luther would have used the three theological virtues of faith, hope, and love from 1 Corinthians 13:13. But while there are places throughout his writings where Luther addressed them individually, he did not provide a systematic treatment of the three theological virtues as a unit.

Instead, when Luther discussed the specific dispositions of Christian virtue, he almost always spoke of qualities that are oriented toward the neighbor, such as kindness, generosity, and goodness. Luther preferred one particular list from Scripture to exemplify the distinctive virtues of the Christian life: the fruit of the Spirit from Galatians 5:22–23. He wrote,

> Paul does not say "works of the Spirit," as he had said "works of the flesh"; but he adorns these *Christian virtues* with a worthier title and calls them "fruit of the Spirit." For they bring very great benefits and fruit, because those who are equipped with them give glory to God and by these virtues invite others to the teaching and faith of Christ.[7]

For Luther, when love appears in the life of the believer, it takes the form of the fruit of the Spirit. Love manifests specifically as joy, peace, patience, kindness, goodness, faithfulness, gentleness, and self-control—those particular virtuous qualities that Scripture promises the Spirit will bring and which are oriented toward care of the neighbor. When Luther referenced the fruit of the Spirit in his writings, which he often did, he frequently called them virtues or even simply referred to them as good works. In his *Exposition of the Lord's Prayer*, he wrote:

> We pattern ourselves after the Father and all his ways . . . *for the names of all virtues are also names given to God.* And since we are baptized into these names and are consecrated and hallowed by them, and since they have thus become our names, it follows that God's children should be called and also be *gentle, merciful, chaste, just, truthful, guileless, friendly, peaceful, and kindly* disposed toward all, even toward our enemies.[8]

Similarly, in the Large Catechism, he wrote:

> Here again we have God's Word, by which He would encourage us and teach us to do true, noble, and grand works such as *gentleness, patience,* and, in short, *love* and *kindness* to our enemies.[9]

Several pages later, he again referred to some of these same qualities—meekness, patience, love, and kindness—as virtues.[10]

While his terminology was not always consistent or precise, Luther clearly esteemed these characteristics as gifts of the Spirit that form us to be virtuous people in Christ.

Scripture indeed teaches that we, as the people of God, are being renewed in His image day by day (Colossians 3:10). The Holy Spirit is at work on our hearts, molding us and shaping us into Christlike people who are increasingly fit for service to God's kingdom. To help us serve that kingdom well, He develops within us the virtuous habits necessary for carrying out God's commands in Christian love. When the new man daily rises, when the person the Spirit is creating us to be shines forth in our lives, it looks like the dispositions of the fruit of the Spirit. This doesn't happen automatically though; we must intentionally embrace these qualities in order to carry out God's command to love our neighbor. Living as baptized people means actively cultivating these virtues in order to continually slay the old sinful nature, those residual pockets of vice and unbelief in our hearts that hinder our ability to live as the holy people God has called us to be.

REFLECTION QUESTIONS

1. What do you think of when you hear the word *virtue*? What does it mean when someone is described as "virtuous"?

2. Read the parable of the Pharisee and the tax collector from Luke 18:9–14. What is one danger when we consider the virtues we strive to exhibit in life? Now read Luke 17:7–10. How does it tell us to consider our virtuous acts?

3. Read Galatians 5:22–23 and John 15:1–8. Which specific qualities will the Spirit bring forth in our lives? What is the key to bearing fruit for the kingdom of God?

4 Read Colossians 3:12–17. How are these virtuous qualities similar to the fruit of the Spirit?

5. Read 2 Peter 1:5–11. What does Peter say we should strive to "add" to our faith? What do these virtuous qualities help us do? How does practicing these qualities add to the sureness of our calling in Christ?

CHAPTER 5

VICE AND VIRTUE

CONTOURS OF GOD'S COMMANDS

How Best to Confess?

If you know much about the Reformation, you will be familiar with Luther's war on penance, the medieval church practice of "working off" sins after confessing them to a priest. The church of Luther's time taught that humans could work toward righteousness before God by avoiding vice and confessing any sins they committed. To help Christians in this endeavor, the church developed exhaustive lists of sins to confess.

But Luther realized that such lists hurt more than they helped. They put an "intolerable burden and weight . . . upon the Christian community," torturing consciences with the "enumeration of all kinds of sin that no one was able to confess purely enough." Luther saw two problems with this practice. One problem occurred when Christians began to trust in the robustness of their confessions rather than "him who promised forgiveness to those who confess."[1] The opposite problem occurred when faithful Christians fretted that they had not confessed thoroughly enough, again calling into question the power of God's forgiveness.

However, Luther also knew that proper repentance requires a specific diagnosis of one's sin to prepare the heart to receive the assurance of the Gospel. To accomplish this, Luther advocated for a simpler version of confession—one that relied on Scripture and trusted in God's promise of forgiveness instead of our own attempts to work off our sin. Rather than a "tedious catalogue" of sin that obscured the Gospel, Luther pointed Christians to the Ten Commandments as a "simple Christian form of prayer and mirror for recognizing sin."[2]

Vice and the Ten Commandments

Luther's counsel was uncomplicated: "We begin with the commandments and there learn to perceive our sin and wickedness, that is, our spiritual sickness which prevents us from doing or leaving undone as we ought." The Ten Commandments are helpful because they "undoubtedly contain all sins if understood correctly." In particular, Luther pointed out that the seven deadly sins are already included in the Decalogue (another name for the Ten Commandments), negating a need for the exhaustive lists that plagued the church of his day:

> Pride [is] in the First and Second, lust in the Sixth, wrath and hatred in the Fifth, gluttony in the Sixth, sloth in the Third, and for that matter, in all of them.[3]

Luther also urged penitent Christians to examine their consciences in the context of the Ten Commandments, not merely in outward word or deed but also in the heart. As Jesus showed in Matthew 5, where He equated anger with murder and lust with adultery, the Commandments address both outward sins and inner transgressions of the heart. While Luther acknowledged that such sins of the heart need not be confessed unless acted upon, he encouraged us to recognize the sinful vice within when we do confess outward deeds against the Commandments:[4]

> For example, regarding the commandment, "Thou shall not commit adultery," one should quickly say

in what manner he has succumbed to *lust* be it by deed, word, or consent, as though he were describing himself completely. . . . Likewise, regarding the commandment, "You shall not kill," one should quickly say by what kind of *anger* he had sinned, whether by hate, slander, cursing, or by the deed itself. And so on with the rest, as I have tried hard to show in my . . . notes on the Decalogue.[5]

Based on this thinking and how Luther treated the vices elsewhere in his writings, consider the following pairings of vices with commandments.

VICE	COMMANDMENT
Greed	Protecting Possessions (7, 9, 10)
Envy	Upholding Reputation (8)
Lust/Gluttony	Sanctifying Sexuality (6)
Wrath/Anger	Supporting Life (5)
Wrath/Anger	Honoring God's Representatives (4)
Sloth	Esteeming God's Word (3)
Pride	Trusting in the True God (1, 2)

Luther's simple categorization helps us see how various vices hinder us as we attempt to carry out the good works related to specific commandments. The pairings are not exclusive—as Luther himself said, sloth can be present in each of the commandments—

and any number of vices can affect good works of various kinds. Nevertheless, it is generally true that one particular vice seems to pair well with each commandment. For example, when it comes to upholding the reputation of others, the vice of envy often leads to gossip, a primary hindrance to the task of the Eighth Commandment.

For Luther, then, the Ten Commandments were a readily available mirror found within Scripture for Christians to see the sin in our lives. By absorbing the categories of vice into our examination, the Decalogue allows us to examine even the innermost recesses of the sinful heart, probing deeper than only our outward transgressions.

Virtue and the Ten Commandments

When considering what shape our outward deeds should take, Luther saw the Decalogue as the gold standard for Christian living—the most comprehensive guide to good works in the Christian life. He grounds this counsel in Christ's own teaching:

> Whoever wants to know what good works are . . . needs to know nothing more than God's commandments. . . . When the young man in Matthew 19[:16–22] asks what he should do to inherit eternal life, Christ sets before him nothing else but the Ten Commandments. Accordingly, we have to learn to recognize good works from the commandments of God."[6]

On every occasion when Luther instructed Christian believers on the shape of good works, invariably he turned to the Decalogue.

This commitment to the commands of God as the guide for Christian behavior means that acquiring virtue is not an end in and of itself. If we consider virtue to be akin to the fruit of the Spirit, as Luther did, then any virtuous disposition is only preliminary; our virtue must find its end in serving the neighbor in the specific ways God has commanded. The virtues then, like the vices, can be readily paired with specific commandments, which they serve to facilitate. For instance, the virtue of kindness, while applicable in every instance of the outward working of Christian love and service to the neighbor, is especially called for when we endeavor, as Luther exhorts in his explanation of the Eighth Commandment in the Small Catechism, to defend our neighbor, "speak well of him, and explain everything in the kindest way." Appropriately, kindness asserts itself as the virtue we especially embrace while carrying out this particular command of God to uphold the reputation of others.

The following pairings of virtues and commandments will guide part 2 of this book. Many of the virtues listed are the familiar names of the fruit of the Spirit. Other virtues in this list trace their origin to the beginning of the vice and virtue tradition. We'll consider how all of these virtues hang together and inform our understanding of the battle against vice in the following chapter. As with the vices, these are not rigid associations but rather helpful pairings that naturally arise when we consider the good works that each commandment calls forth.

VIRTUE	COMMANDMENT
Generosity/Goodness	Protecting Possessions (7, 9, 10)
Kindness	Upholding Reputation (8)
Chastity/Temperance/ Self-Control	Sanctifying Sexuality (6)
Peace/Gentleness/ Forgiveness	Supporting Life (5)
Patience	Honoring God's Representatives (4)
Diligence/Zeal	Esteeming God's Word (3)
Humility	Trusting in the True God (1, 2)

By pairing these virtues with the commandments, we see the true purpose of Christian virtue: to serve the neighbor in concrete works of love. This is the difference between how the pagan philosophy of Aristotle viewed virtue and how Luther knew the church should understand virtue. When the disposition of the virtues are prized in and of themselves, too often the neighbor in need is forgotten. For a virtue to have value, it must result in serving the neighbor, lest the pursuit of virtue become an egotistical striving for recognition.

Luther noted this in his *Personal Prayer Book* as he discussed the good works called for in the Fourth through Tenth Commandments:

> In all such actions we see nothing but a strange, all-comprehending love toward God and our neighbor which never seeks its own advantage but only what serves God and our neighbor [1 Cor. 13:5]. It means to devote oneself freely to belonging to one's neighbor and serving him and his concerns. . . . We have clearly emphasized that these commandments prescribe nothing that man is to do or leave undone for his own advantage, or expect of others for himself, but rather what a person is to do or leave undone toward his neighbor, toward God, and toward his fellowman. Therefore we must comprehend the fulfilment of the commandments as meaning love for others and not for ourselves.[7]

For Luther, a "truly Christian life" means to live for others, that all our actions "may serve and benefit" them and not ourselves.[8]

Contours of God's Commands

When Luther instructed Christians on the meaning of the Decalogue, he regularly used vice and virtue to fill out the particular contours of each of the Ten Commandments. As noted by Albrecht Peters in his comprehensive commentary on the catechisms, Luther focused his "interpretation of the commandment on the vice to be combated and the virtue commanded that helps to overcome it."[9] In other words, Luther used opposite pairings of vices and virtues to shape his presentation of the Ten Commandments.

We see a subtle version of this practice in the brief explanations of the Commandments in Luther's Small Catechism. In the Fourth Commandment, we are taught not to provoke our parents to *anger*. In the Sixth, we are exhorted to lead a *chaste* and decent life, and *kindness* is associated with keeping the Eighth Commandment. This method is even more evident in the longer explanations found in the Large Catechism. When Luther explained the Fifth Commandment, he noted the importance of learning to be *gentle* and *patient* in order to restrain our desire for revenge.[10]

Luther's pattern of prohibiting vice and encouraging the cultivation of the virtues for good works appears not only in his catechisms but also in most every place where he teaches on the Decalogue or provides instruction on how to make confession. The following chart provides a simple illustration of Luther's pattern. While not exhaustive, the groupings summarize the intersection of vice and virtue within the context of the Decalogue and will help us explore how Luther saw vice and virtue at work in the life of the baptized.

COMMANDMENT	VICE (-)	VIRTUE (+)
Protecting Possessions (7, 9, 10)	Greed	Generosity/Goodness
Upholding Reputation (8)	Envy	Kindness
Sanctifying Sexuality (6)	Lust/Gluttony	Chastity/Temperance/ Self-Control
Supporting Life (5)	Wrath/Anger	Peace/Gentleness/ Forgiveness
Honoring God's Representatives (4)	Wrath/Anger	Patience
Esteeming God's Word (3)	Sloth	Diligence/Zeal
Trusting in the True God (1, 2)	Pride	Humility

REFLECTION QUESTIONS

1. Read the Ten Commandments from *Exodus* 20:3–17 or Deuteronomy 5:7–21. What does each commandment forbid? What does each protect or promote?

2. What does Jesus teach that those who love Him will do? See John 14:15; 15:10.

3. In the parable of the rich young man in Matthew 19:16–22, Jesus offers a guide for living. What does Jesus' list echo?

4. Read Matthew 22:34–40. What does Jesus say are the two greatest commandments? Which of the Ten Commandments relate to loving God? Which relate to loving our neighbor?

5. Read Romans 13:8–10 and Galatians 5:14. How do we fulfill the Law? What does love look like according to Paul? Who is the primary recipient of our good works? How does keeping each of the Ten Commandments specifically serve our neighbor in love?

CHAPTER 6

KILLING UNBELIEF

SLAYING THE OLD MAN DAY BY DAY

The Battlefield of the Soul

Imagine you are standing on a vast battlefield. As you gaze out upon the horizon, a warrior appears. You recognize this adversary: the vice of envy, flashing forth images of the good life that all your friends seem to enjoy. Covetous desire rises from within with each enemy attack; you need to put up a defense. But which arrow from your quiver shall you select for such a foe? You reach back and draw the one most fit to slay this opponent, unleashing the virtue of kindness upon the approaching tyrant, and then watch your foe fall to the ground. You were prepared for this fight because lately you have intentionally worked to celebrate the success of others instead of envying them.

Before you can relish your victory, another war cry sounds. Charging at your flank is a different warrior who goes by the name of wrath, a vice you often struggle with when your temper gets the best of you. You wince, a bit unprepared for the coming clash, but eventually heft your shield of the virtue of patience to deflect the blow of this angry combatant. Who, you wonder, will the commander of these enemy forces send next?

Such is the daily battle in our soul as vice and virtue contend for the allegiance of our heart. Perhaps you haven't envisioned it that way, but the ancients often used a battlefield to describe this reality. The example above was inspired by a fourth-century Spanish Christian named Prudentius, who depicted a dreamlike battle between Christian virtues and worldly vices in his work *Psychomachia*, which literally means "soul warfare." (While you may not have heard of Prudentius, you have probably sung a hymn he wrote—"Of the Father's Love Begotten"!)

Likewise, Gregory the Great, the one who finalized the list we know as the seven deadly sins, described how vices mount an onslaught against our souls:

> For the tempting vices, which fight against us in invisible contest in behalf of the pride which reigns over them, some of them go first, like captains, others follow, after the manner of an army. . . . For when pride, the queen of sins, has fully possessed a conquered heart, she surrenders it immediately to seven principal sins, as if to some of her generals, to lay it waste. And an army in truth follows these generals, because, doubtless, there spring up from them importunate hosts of sins. . . . But seven principal vices, as its first progeny, spring doubtless from this poisonous root, namely, vain glory, envy, anger, melancholy, avarice, gluttony, lust.[1]

Here Gregory details how pride acts as a commanding general, sending other vices forth into battle, and illustrates how the capital vices have a generative power in giving birth to other sin. Such "offspring vices," as they are known, proceed from the capital vices like captains under their general and do battle against vulnerable human hearts.

Battle imagery like that supplied by Prudentius, Gregory, and others within the vice tradition provides a clue regarding the best way to fight sin. To be effective in the fight against sin, we must cut it off at the root! The Fifth Commandment's prohibition against murder, for instance, is hardly effective if we do not deal with the vice of anger that precedes the act of murder. This is why Jesus equates anger with murder in the Sermon on the Mount—anger is murder in the heart.

But how do we go about contending against a vice like anger, or any of the others? What is the best strategy to win the battle? For the ancients, the best bet against any given vice was to repeatedly practice the opposite virtue. Against anger, practice patience and forgiveness; against greed, practice generosity; and so on. The virtues that counteract the seven capital vices are often referred to as the contrarian virtues, because they act contrary to some corresponding vicious behavior. This virtue tradition aligns well with the scriptural virtues of the fruit of the Spirit, which were Luther's preferred way to describe virtue.

The following chart tracks the correlation between the capital vices, their opposite virtues, and the related fruit of the Spirit. Some connections are obvious. Others become clear with a little study—for example, the Greek word translated as "goodness" in Galatians 5:22 carries the connotation of generosity, which is why it corresponds to charity. While not exclusive pairings, these general associations help us understand how to employ virtuous dispositions in the battle of our own soul.

VICE	CONTRARY VIRTUE	FRUIT OF THE SPIRIT
Pride	Humility	Gentleness
Envy	Kindness	Kindness
Anger	Patience, Forgiveness	Patience, Peace
Sloth	Diligence or Zeal	Love, Joy
Greed	Generosity or Charity	Goodness
Gluttony	Temperance	Self-Control
Lust	Chastity	

Luther on the Fight of Faith

What is at stake in this fight? Why did the ancients picture grand battles over things like sloth and envy in the human soul? Luther knew the answer: because vices are not just "bad habits," and virtues are not just "good habits." The movement from vice to virtue is a movement from unbelief to belief, from being enslaved to ourselves and our passions to being free to serve our neighbor in need. Paul calls this war the "fight of the faith" (1 Timothy 6:12), and Luther taught that engaging in this battle each day is the essence of living baptized.

Luther frequently warned about the danger of works-righteousness—a core tenet of Reformation theology. And it's true; our works cannot save us. However, Luther regarded something else as even more dangerous to the Christian's soul. A worse danger, he contended, is to assume we have forgiveness without repentance:

> Many now talk only about the forgiveness of sins and say little or nothing about repentance. There neither is forgiveness of sins without repentance nor can forgiveness of sins be understood without repentance. It follows that if we preach the forgiveness of sins without repentance that the people imagine that they have already obtained the forgiveness of sins, becoming thereby secure and without compunction of conscience. This would be a *greater error and sin than all the errors hitherto prevailing.* Surely we need to be concerned lest, as Christ says in Matt. 12[:45] the last state becomes worse than the first.[2]

Works-righteousness comprised the "first state," indeed an intolerable offense to the true Gospel. But the greater danger is the "last state," the false security that occurs when we spurn the repentance faith requires. A person living with a terrified conscience from a works-righteousness understanding of salvation can ultimately land and rest secure on the grace of Jesus Christ. But those who are confident of God's grace while living a life controlled by idolatrous vice proceed to their doom tragically unaware.

Here, too, the Scriptures drove Luther's convictions. For example, interpreting 1 Corinthians 13, Luther pointed out that the Corinthians who practiced faith without works of love had a "false faith" and, like many in his own day, were "Christians in name only" for true faith is never idle. The clarity of God's Word on the matter allowed Luther to confidently declare that "anyone may very easily try and find out whether he is a Christian and a true believer in Christ" by "whether he is doing good works or not."[3] The reformer understood that genuine faith always manifests in good works, including repentance.[4]

As Luther witnessed Christians flaunting their freedom in Christ, he warned them that genuine faith does not exist without contrition—that is, recognizing one's sin and turning from it. Luther called it a "shameful vice" when Christians think we have no need of repentance and persist in "security and contentment" despite our sin.[5] Christians whose lives display persistent and unrepented vice have reason for alarm. Assumed security in Christ without regard for how we conduct our lives is a false security, as Luther bluntly stated:

> There is no such Christ that died for sinners who do not, after the forgiveness of sins, desist from sins and lead a new life. . . . He who does not abstain from sin, but persists in his evil life, must have a different Christ. . . . The real Christ is not there. . . . He must be damned with this, his new Christ.[6]

Some might wonder whether Luther is being a bit overzealous, given his corresponding emphasis on the assurance of salvation believers have in Christ Jesus. But Luther consistently warned the faithful about the danger of falling away from faith by allowing sin to thrive in their lives. Luther was certain: we must "battle unceasingly against sin, to destroy it," and if we do not, "we shall relish neither Christ nor God."[7] Luther never let his confidence in the Gospel blind him to sin's ability to destroy faith.

When Christians allow sin to rule in them, we risk hell itself! The devil comes "pushing and provoking in all directions" to bring us "into misbelief, false security, and stubbornness," and so Luther exhorted Christians "to cry out and to pray that God would not allow us to become weary and faint and to fall again into sin, shame, and unbelief."[8]

Slaying the Old Man

For true Christians, the fight of faith against sin is not an option. We read in Scripture that we must "abstain from the passions of the flesh, which wage war against your soul" (1 Peter 2:11) and that we must not let sin "reign in your mortal body, to make you obey its passions" (Romans 6:12). "In these and like passages," Luther wrote, "we are shown that nobody is without evil lust, but that everybody should and must fight against it daily." Luther painted his own picture of our battle—describing how the flesh, the world, and the devil have "hemmed us in with . . . powerful and mighty armies"—and called on us to fight these enemies.[9]

Once Christians have commended their souls to Christ in faith, our next focus must be "the discipline of the flesh, the *killing* of its gross evil lust." Luther recognized that, according to our old nature, "'man's heart and mind incline always to evil,' that is, to *pride . . . anger, hatred, covetousness*, etc. . . . If God is to live and work in him, all this vice and wickedness must be choked and uprooted."[10] Because these vices are equivalent to idolatry, the call to put them to death is ultimately a call to kill our unbelief. While our new nature in Christ will freely desire to engage in this battle, the old man continually seeks to thwart these efforts.

Therefore, Luther urged that man "must learn to do not what his own will wants him to do, but always to do what runs counter to his will. He must always work against his will."[11] In other words, we must intentionally engage in practices that run counter to sinful desires. In this way, our will to sin is broken and we are freed to live within God's will. For Luther, this is how we live out our Baptism:

> God makes this struggle between our flesh and our spirit, with their contradictory desires, *the task of all whom he causes to be baptized and called.* . . . This means that spirit and flesh strive against one another, but the spirit shall prevail, though only with difficulty and hard work, and shall put down the disobedient flesh, as St. Paul says in Gal. 5[:24], "All who are Christians or belong to Christ crucify the flesh with its lusts and *vices.*" . . . Ceaselessly we must fight against *avarice, unchastity, anger,* and ambition. Steadfastly and with toil and sorrow we must wrestle with carnal desires.[12]

The nature of the fight is clear. We are called to kill the idolatrous vices that lurk in our sinful hearts, to kill our unbelief, to slay the old man day by day that our faith might live.

Fighting alongside the Spirit

But wait, you might be wondering, is this fight really my responsibility? Isn't the Holy Spirit the one who gets all the credit for my becoming more holy? If this is your first inclination, you would be at least partly correct. Luther consistently answered that the battle of the soul is fought by the power of the Holy Spirit.[13] He wrote:

> [When the Word is preached,] God supplies the Spirit and performs powerful deeds in the hearers. Similarly, Paul says here [in Galatians 3:5] that God has supplied the Spirit to the Galatians and has performed powerful deeds among them. . . . "By the same power of the Spirit you, who used to be *covetous, adulterous, angry, impatient, and hostile,* have become *generous, chaste, gentle, patient, and loving* toward your neighbors."[14]

Since the Holy Spirit is the active agent in our sanctification, what, if anything, is left for the Christian to do? Some believe that Luther's view negated any responsibility on the believer's part, that Christians should understand themselves to be entirely passive when it comes to being made holy. Some even accuse Luther,

Lutherans, and other Protestant heirs of being against the very idea of cultivating virtue in the Christian life.

But this is not how Scripture—or Luther—speaks. On one hand, Scripture is clear that God, working through the Holy Spirit, is wholly responsible for our sanctification. But Scripture also clearly states that humans are accountable for our own sanctification. We see both truths in Philippians 2:12–13, for example:

> **Work out your own salvation with fear and trembling, for it is God who works in you, both to will and to work for His good pleasure.**

Here Paul exhorts us to work out our own salvation—the human effort we are accountable for—and then immediately follows with the affirmation that God is the true agent at work in our hearts. We may not easily grasp this paradox with our human reason, but nevertheless it is what Scripture teaches. Both realities must be upheld when we consider what it means to live out our Baptism each day.

Paul elsewhere writes that each of us will give an account for our deeds done in the flesh, whether good or bad (2 Corinthians 5:10), and Jesus says this account will be given on judgment day (Matthew 12:36). When the Scriptures speak about our moral responsibility, they consistently convey that all Christians will ultimately be held accountable for their behavior, how they labored alongside and in the power of the Spirit.

Luther echoed this in his own understanding. In his commentary on Galatians, for example, Luther declared, "It is *up to you* to be diligently on your guard not to use your freedom as an opportunity for the flesh," and yet a few pages later he maintained with Paul that our sanctification is accomplished "by the Spirit."[15]

Since both realities are ongoing—God's working and our own—it is not possible for us to differentiate between the Spirit's work and our own moral striving. One way Luther addressed this mystery was to distinguish between two complementary concepts of God's grace. We usually understand the term *grace* to mean God's favor—that is, grace is what reconciles a believer to God the Father through the work of Jesus Christ. But Luther also spoke of grace as a gift given to the believer as a means to cultivate a holy life. Grace as gift implies active participation on the part of the Christian. The divine grace of God's favor always precedes any human action, but this grace continues to flow through believers, resulting in their righteous activity.[16]

While our sanctification will be incomplete in this life, God's gift of grace will bring transformation in our lives now, as Luther beautifully summarized:

> Christ . . . has purchased redemption from sin and death so that the Holy Spirit might transform us out of the old Adam into new men—we die unto sin and live unto righteousness, beginning and growing here on earth and perfecting it beyond, as St. Paul teaches. Christ did not earn only *gratia*, "grace," for us, but also *donum*, "the gift of the Holy Spirit," so that we might have not only forgiveness of, but also cessation of, sin.[17]

As flesh and Spirit wage war in our souls, believers have a job to do. Luther reminds us that not only does God save real sinners but He also calls on us to mortify our real sins.[18] Each day we must slay the old man within. To live baptized means to awaken each morning and say, "Today I must kill my anger," or "Today I will fight against my lust." If we do not do battle with these remnants of unbelief in our heart, they will grow larger and possibly choke out faith altogether!

But be encouraged: we have the most powerful ally we could ever hope for in this fight of the soul. We have the unsurpassable might of the Holy Spirit on our side. While His weapons might not look mighty to the world, Scripture teaches us they have the power to vanquish strongholds (see 2 Corinthians 10:4). Marching into battle with the Spirit by our side, we will not be afraid.

REFLECTION QUESTIONS

1. Read Ephesians 6:10–20. What does Paul encourage us to do in this passage that we might be ready for battle? Who are our true enemies?

2. Read 1 Peter 2:11–12. What do we learn about the "passions of the flesh" in this passage? What are they attempting to do to our soul? According to Galatians 5:24, what should we do to our passions of the flesh?

3. Read 2 Timothy 2:3–4 and 1 Timothy 6:11–12. What profession does Paul use to describe followers of Jesus Christ? Why might he use this analogy? How do these passages shape our thinking about the spiritual battle?

PART 2

BATTLE OF THE SOUL

This life, therefore, is not godliness but the process of becoming godly, not health but getting well, not being but becoming, not rest but exercise. We are not now what we shall be, but we are on the way. The process is not yet finished, but it is actively going on. This is not the goal but it is the right road. At present, everything does not gleam and sparkle, but everything is being cleansed.

Martin Luther, *Defense and Explanation of All the Articles*

Part 1 explored how Luther reformed the vice and virtue tradition from its philosophical and Scholastic roots for use in Gospel-centered living. In particular, Luther used the concepts of virtue and vice to illustrate the positive and negative sides of the Decalogue at the level of the inner heart, as summarized in the chart at the end of chapter 5.

Based on those connections, we now delve into the precise nature of each commandment and the related vice and virtue—that we might be better armed to fight the battle of the soul. Each chapter focuses on a commandment (or grouping of commandments) and begins by examining the good works that are called for by that commandment. Then we consider both the vice that prevents and the virtue that facilitates those good works as we live out God's commands in our daily life through the power of the Spirit. We will proceed in descending order through the Decalogue, with the exception of the Ninth and Tenth Commandments, which appear with the Seventh Commandment because of their shared emphasis on protecting personal property.

As we fight against the idols of vice, their grip on our hearts is continually loosened, and the new man is freed more and more to embrace those virtues the Holy Spirit is laboring to grow within us. These virtues fit us for service to our neighbor, equipping us for the tasks God has prepared for us.

This war within will not be over until we die in Christ, but we can make real progress as we strive to live baptized. We can foster habits that help us more consistently win our battles with vice. As

Luther wrote, this is the "right road" for every Christian to be on as we march toward our heavenly victory.[1] As you encounter the following chapters, consider practical steps you might take to foster godliness in your life, knowing that God is working to cleanse your soul so that one day it will gleam and sparkle in righteousness and purity forever.

> Put to death therefore what is earthly in you.
>
> (*Colossians 3:5*)

CHAPTER 7

KILLING ENVY:
KINDNESS

The Eighth Commandment
You shall not give false testimony
against your neighbor.

Status by Self

Every vice is rooted in our prideful attempts to take control of our lives—usually prompted by fear. When we are afraid life won't turn out like we want, we try to manipulate our circumstances to get the outcome we hope for. Perhaps nowhere is this more evident than when it comes to how we feel others perceive us as a person. Our reputation with others can seemingly make or break us, regardless whether their opinions are true. When we think our status with others has somehow been diminished, we find ourselves doing things we never thought we'd do to regain good standing. This is the vice of envy at its ugliest.

Think back to a time when you felt left out. Maybe some friends threw a party and you didn't make the invite list. Maybe you were the star of the team until another kid moved to town and bumped you to the bench. Maybe you thought you were in line for a promotion, but it went to your colleague instead. How did you feel? How did you respond?

Moments like these can make us feel worthless. They can make us seethe at the person we perceive has displaced us. At our worst, we might even try to diminish that person's reputation in an attempt to reestablish our own—in other words, we break the Eighth Commandment.

The Eighth Commandment—Reputation

We all know how difficult it is to live in community when our reputation has been broken. Sometimes we do things that justly damage how others view and subsequently interact with us. Bad choices harm relationships, and it takes a lot of work and time to restore our reputation afterward. It's all the more devastating when someone damages our reputation unjustly. That's what the Eighth Commandment is designed to protect: reputations.

"God does not want the reputation, good name, and upright character of our neighbor to be taken away or diminished. . . . He wants everyone to stand in his integrity before wife, children, servants, and neighbors," Luther wrote.[1] Telling lies is the primary way to unjustly damage another's reputation, so God in His wisdom attempts to protect our neighbor's reputation through the Eighth Commandment's prohibition against bearing false witness.

While the most direct application of this commandment is in the context of giving a true witness before a court of law, Luther recognized that "this commandment forbids all sins of the tongue . . . by which we may injure or confront our neighbor."[2] Our speech is the weapon we most often employ to damage our neighbor's reputation. Therefore, in the Small Catechism, Luther summarized the positive aspect of this commandment's explanation by teaching that we are not to "tell lies about our neighbor, betray him, slander him, or hurt his reputation, but defend him, speak well of him, and explain everything in the kindest way."

Sometimes Christians will become aware of legitimate sins of others. In these cases, Luther reasoned, while we may "indeed see and hear that [our] neighbor sins . . . [we] have no command to report it to others." Rather, Luther pointed Christians to our

Lord's instructions for dealing with sin in Matthew 18 and instructed: "Let this, then, be your rule, that you do not too quickly spread evil about your neighbor and slander him to others. Instead, admonish him privately that he may amend his life." Further, not only are we to avoid spreading gossip, but "if you meet an idle tongue that betrays and slanders someone, contradict such a person promptly to his face, . . . so he may blush."[3] Thus, this precept calls for vigilance over both the words we speak and the words we hear.

Luther concluded his treatment of the good work that is called for in the Eighth Commandment with these words:

> Now we have the sum and general understanding of this commandment: Let no one do any harm to his neighbor with the tongue, whether friend or foe. Do not speak evil of him, no matter whether it is true or false, unless it is done by commandment or for his reformation. Let everyone use his tongue and make it serve for the best of everyone else, to cover up his neighbor's sins and infirmities . . . , excuse them, conceal and garnish them with his own reputation.[4]

Envy

What condition of the heart would lead a person to deliberately sully another's reputation? One answer is envy. Few things

BATTLE *OF THE* **SOUL**

hinder our ability to uphold reputations like envy. Luther explicitly made this connection:

> When your neighbor sees that you have a better house and home, ‹a larger family and more fertile fields,› greater possessions and fortune from God than he does, he gets in a bad mood, *envies* you, and speaks no good of you. So by the devil's encouragement you will get many enemies who cannot bear to see you have any good, either bodily or spiritual.[5]

The most basic definition of envy in the vice tradition is to have sorrow over another's good.[6] When we see the success of our neighbors, we desire what is rightfully theirs, which naturally leads us to want to tear them down. When we constantly think that others have it better, we feel more and more useless. We want the life they have. Envy does not just want others' things—a focus on acquiring "stuff" is more characteristic of greed. Rather, envy seeks the status those possessions provide. We aren't content to drive the same kind of car as our neighbor; we want our neighbor to drive a car that is inferior to our own! Envy becomes particularly dangerous when our desire to have a greater status leads us to take malicious actions against others. Luther cautioned against this:

> We must know that God does not want you to deprive your neighbor of anything that belongs to him, so that he suffer the loss. . . . This is true even if you could keep it honorably before the world. For

it is a secret and sly trick done "under the hat," as we say, so it may not be noticed. Although you go your way as if you had done no one any wrong, you have still injured your neighbor. If it is not called stealing and cheating, it is still called coveting your neighbor's property, that is, aiming at possession of it, luring it away from him without his consent, and *being unwilling to see him enjoy what God has granted him.*[7]

In the ancient Near East, to begrudge what another had was to cast an "evil eye" upon them, a shameful practice to be avoided. In the parable of the laborers in the vineyard in Matthew 20:1–16, Jesus uses this exact terminology in verse 15: "Am I not allowed to do what I choose with what belongs to me? Or is your eye evil because I am good?" Most Bible translations render it similar to the English Standard Version, "Or do you begrudge my generosity?" which obscures the connection to the idiom of the envious evil eye. The Germans even developed a specific word for what envy means: *schadenfreude*, which is literally rendered "sorrow-joy" and means to rejoice when a rival's reputation, life, or property is damaged.

The ancients recognized—as do people today—that attempts to sabotage our rivals usually start with gossip and slander. In other words, envy directly influences us to break the Eighth Commandment. Luther shared this observation, frequently calling attention to one of envy's most infamous offspring sins: gossip, or what he called backbiting. He noted that the Eighth Commandment "applies especially to the detestable, shameless vice of backbiting or slander" and described its consequences: "Learning a bit of gossip about someone else, they spread it into every corner. . . . Though you do not wield a sword, you use your venomous tongue to bring disgrace and harm upon your neighbor."[8]

Envy does even more damage. We harm our neighbor through envious gossip, of course, but we also harm ourselves. Proverbs 14:30 says, "Envy makes the bones rot." Commenting on Titus 3:3, Luther said that people who "pine away with envy . . . will be consumed with the most evil thoughts, and are their own worst cross."[9] By obsessing over what others have and their status, we ruin our own mental health and create struggles for ourselves, sometimes even affecting our physical health.

We also cause spiritual damage to ourselves. When we envy others and hate them because of their status compared to our own, whom are we really mad at? The only honest answer is God Himself. We might lash out against our neighbor, but that's only because they can be reached by our thoughts, words, and actions in a way that God seemingly can't. Our real problem is with God—thinking that He has unfairly doled out our lot in life, that we deserve better. We don't trust God to provide the happiness we desperately desire, and so we take matters into our own hands.

At heart, envy is a manifestation of idolatry. We play God, clinging to ourselves as a better god than the Creator. But we cannot engineer our status, and we end up ruining both our neighbor and ourselves in that futile quest.

Kindness

The virtue tradition knew that we combat the vice of envy with kindness. Preaching on 1 Peter, Luther said: "If I suppress hatred and envy, I become all the more willing to be kind and friendly to my neighbor." Interpreting the word *kindness* in Galatians 5:22, Luther wrote:

> This means a *gentleness* and sweetness in manner and in one's entire life. For Christians should not be harsh and morose; they should be gentle, humane, affable, courteous, people with whom others enjoy associating, people who overlook the mistakes of others or *put the best construction on them.*[10]

Luther closely associated kindness and gentleness, and both are fruit of the Spirit. Several Greek words can be translated to "gentleness," and Luther commented on two of them to show how they work against envy:

> *Prautes* [gentleness] is that noblest of virtues which does not become angry. . . . Here [in Titus 3, Paul] sets some vices over against the virtues so that on the basis of these you might understand what he means by *epieikeia* [gentleness/fairness] and courtesy. We should, he says, bear the malicious acts of others. Why? Look behind you. If you see how your envy is tolerated and how those who are compelled to put up with your envy behave, you should act the same way toward that of others.[11]

Here Luther carefully reasoned about how the mutual connotations of certain vices and virtues inform our understanding of them. This helps the Christian discern which behaviors are being warned against and which positive dispositions will help us overcome that vice.

The contours of the Eighth Commandment far exceed a basic prohibition against lying. Luther expanded its application, calling our attention to the nature of speech and the importance of preserving our neighbor's reputation in the community. An envious heart deters us from maintaining our neighbor's good standing and drives us to gossip, slander, and malice, as Luther understood. Thus, Luther acknowledged the need to cultivate kindness in our actions and attitudes in order to uphold the Eighth Commandment.

Envy destroys relationships and reputations. It wants others to be as unhappy as we are. Envy would rather we both have nothing than to see our neighbor better off. Envy is a form of unbelief that does not trust God will provide what I need to be content. If we allow it to persist in our lives, the unbelief behind envy may cause us to lose our faith in God altogether. Envy must therefore be killed.

As baptized children of God, we wake each day and fight the envy in our hearts. In its place, we allow the kindness wrought by the Spirit to guide our interactions with family, friends, and neighbors. We embrace the virtue of kindness to help us keep God's command to uphold the reputation of our neighbors, to celebrate their successes, and to love them as God has loved us.

REFLECTION QUESTIONS

1. Think of a time in your life when you envied someone. How much did it affect you? Did it ever drive you to treat them badly or say bad things about them? What happened as a result?

2. Think of some examples in Scripture of strife between people—for instance, Cain and Abel (Genesis 4), Joseph and his brothers (Genesis 37), or Ahab and Naboth (1 Kings 21). How might the vice of envy have been at play in these scenarios?

3. Read Jesus' parable of the laborers in the vineyard in Matthew 20:1–16. How does comparing ourselves to others give rise to discontentment? Who is the true distributor of wealth and status? According to Philippians 4:11–13, where can Christians turn to find contentment?

4. We often act on envy by slandering others. Read James 3:5–12. What is the danger in allowing our tongues to speak evil of others? How is this inconsistent with the Christian life?

5. Read Philippians 2:3–4. What does Paul recommend in place of "selfish ambition or conceit"? How does considering others before ourselves help fight against the vice of envy?

CHAPTER 8

KILLING GREED:
GENEROSITY

The Tenth Commandment

You shall not covet your neighbor's wife, or his manservant or maidservant, his ox or donkey, or anything that belongs to your neighbor.

The Ninth Commandment

You shall not covet your neighbor's house.

The Seventh Commandment

You shall not steal.

To Give or Not to Give?

I'm sure you've been there—walking down the street of some big city, admiring the magnificent buildings and all the trappings of a wealthy society. Then you round a corner and there sits a person who is homeless, downcast, holding a crude cardboard sign and begging for change. Perhaps you've thought, How can such wealth and poverty exist side by side? How can there be multimillionaires in high rises just above a street where people are literally starving to death?

Let me ask you: Did you give to that person? I admit, I rarely do. I assuage my conscience by assuming things that I really don't know. I assume that this person made bad choices to end up on the street and that it is not my responsibility to remedy the consequences of their decisions. I tell myself, "I'm where I'm at in life because I worked hard and made different choices." But deep down, I know that circumstances in my life could just as easily have landed me homeless and hungry as well. Deep down, I know I can't take credit for my relative successes.

Maybe it's not so hard to walk past a total stranger for whom we feel little responsibility, but let's bring this closer to home. Say you own a business and you've got an employee who is struggling to make ends meet. You could well afford to give her a raise, but the market doesn't demand it, and of course, it would cut into your profit. Or maybe your brother-in-law lost his job, and he's having trouble paying his mortgage while he looks for a new one. It's desperate enough that he asks you for some help until he's in a better spot. You would love to help out, you tell him, but you promised your kids that big vacation this summer and you don't want to go back on your word.

What is at work as we wrestle with these decisions? Money and possessions, no doubt. But writhing beneath the surface is the tension between greed and generosity, between focus on self and focus on others.

Commandments Seven, Nine, and Ten—Possessions and Property

The Seventh, Ninth, and Tenth Commandments show that God sets boundaries around our neighbor's money, property, and possessions in order to protect them. In the Small Catechism, Luther explained that the Seventh Commandment calls us to uphold the integrity of our neighbor's possessions: "We should fear and love God so that we do not take our neighbor's money or possessions, or get them in any dishonest way, but help him improve and protect his possessions and income." Similarly, the Ninth and Tenth Commandments prohibit all coveting in order to protect those things that rightfully belong to another. In his explanation of the Ninth Commandment in the Small Catechism, Luther taught that we are not to "scheme to get our neighbor's inheritance or house, or get it in a way which only appears right, but help and be of service to him in keeping it."

But stealing is not just "emptying our neighbor's money box and pockets," Luther knew. Christians continuously apply God's foundational Ten Commands—in this case, not to steal or covet—to guide us in our particular situations. Luther extended the Seventh Commandment to include "avarice, fraudulent gain, deceit, craftiness, or allowing harm to happen to or hindering our neighbor's keeping what belongs to him." For example, laziness could be considered stealing when we waste time while earning a wage.[1] Taking advantage of others with "clever tricks" such as overcharging them or greedily driving a hard bargain could also be considered stealing. The overarching principle of the commands that protect another's belongings is this: a person "must do no harm to his neighbor nor deprive him of profit nor commit any act of unfaithfulness or hatred in any bargain or trade. But he must also faithfully preserve his property for him, secure and promote his advantage."[2]

Greed

Not surprisingly, the vice of greed causes the most trouble in this area. Luther situated his entire discussion of the Seventh Commandment around greed, a vice he considered so widespread that it was "practically futile to preach against it."[3] As commentator Albrecht Peters observed, Luther placed "the prohibition of stealing under this scope: the holy zealous God watches over our human community and protects the possessions of our neighbor against infringements of our greed."[4] In our modern, capitalist context, greed has at times been understood in a positive sense. But in the vice tradition and in Scripture, greed is a negative quality. Thomas Aquinas defined greed as an excessive love of or desire for money or any possession money can buy.[5] Greed (or avarice, a closely related term) means always wanting to have more, constantly accumulating or retaining wealth and possessions.

Greed is particularly linked with idolatry. In Ephesians 5:5 and Colossians 3:5, Paul includes lists of sins, and both lists equate covetousness with idolatry. Luther made special note of this and therefore emphasized that Paul "calls no other sin idolatry except covetousness . . . because this sin shows most starkly that a man does not trust God for anything, but expects more benefit from his money than from God."[6] While Luther and Paul knew that all sin is, at base, idolatry, they highlight that this is most easily seen when we grasp at wealth for security. Jesus Himself points out this reality when He said it is impossible for a person to serve both God and money at the same time (Matthew 6:24).

Luther considered money the most common idol on earth, and he warned that this kind of idolatry is especially deceitful because "greed has a very pretty and attractive cover for its shame; it is called provision for the body and the needs of nature."[7] We like to pretend our greed is simply love for our family, a desire to be wise with money and have enough to supply our basic needs. After all, Paul also writes that "if anyone does not provide for his relatives, and especially for members of his household, he has denied the faith and is worse than an unbeliever" (1 Timothy 5:8). Jesus rebuked the Pharisees who felt it was more important to give money to God than to care for their elderly parents (Mark 7:8–13). But often we are masking the real reason behind our desire to keep what we have and gather more: we do not trust that God will provide for us. Ultimately, Luther saw greed as a sign of unbelief, in opposition to faith that trusts in God's gracious aid.[8]

Instead of bringing security or provision, greed actually increases our trouble in life because of its insatiable nature. Luther wrote:

> The more money acquired, the greater the greed. Man can never be sated with wealth; but his appetite for it grows and grows. The same is true of all other evil human lusts. The more honor a man receives, the more he covets. The more land and power, the greater the desire to increase these. . . . If [the human heart] possessed the entire world, it would like to have two worlds; if it had two, it would like to have ten. . . . Therefore we must not give thought to finding ways to satisfy greed. . . . No, *greed must be killed.*[9]

Even if we get what we want, we will never actually be happy or satisfied:

> Those who have used all their care and diligence to gather great possessions and wealth, what have they finally gained? You will find that they have wasted their toil and labor, or even though they have amassed great treasures, they have been dispersed and scattered. . . . So they themselves have never found happiness in their wealth.[10]

Finally, greed also does harm to our neighbor who relies on our gracious aid. When we are in the grip of greed, we are concerned only with our own accumulation. We lose sight of our neighbors in need. Luther wrote that "covetousness and concern for this world's goods hinder the gospel greatly from bearing fruit," choking out the Word of God "so that it proves unfruitful," as described in Matthew 13:22.[11] Our hoarding of more nearly always means some neighbor in our midst is doing without. Greedily taking more than our share violates the principle of justice and harms the underprivileged and less fortunate around us.

In his own context, Luther particularly applied this to usury, the practice of lending money with exorbitant interest. For Luther, this practice promoted the vice of greed and the accumulation of wealth at the expense of the neighbor: "Because of [the lender's] avarice, therefore, goods must be priced as much higher as the greater need of the other fellow will allow, so that the neighbor's need becomes . . . the measure of the goods' worth and value."[12] Here, our greed causes us to exploit our neighbor in need under the pretense of a fair business dealing.

We strive to overcome greed, then, not just to guard our hearts from unbelief and obey God's commands but also to serve our neighbor in love.

Generosity

Prominent Luther scholar Robert Kolb observes that material blessings can function in one of two ways in our lives. Commonly, they serve as a source of temptation and lead us into idolatry. However, they need not do so. Our excess provision can also enable us to support our neighbors in need.[13] He points our attention to Luther's observations to his congregation in 1531: "It is no sin to have money and property, wife and children, house and home. But you must not let it be your master. You must make it serve you, and you must be its master."[14]

The way to kill our greed is to practice generosity. When we give away some of what God has given to us, we show our trust in His ability to provide for our needs again in the future. Therefore, Luther described the virtuous, positive work of the Seventh Commandment in terms of generosity: when a person trusts God, "he does not cling to money; he uses his money cheerfully and freely for the benefit of his neighbor. He knows full well that he will have enough no matter how much he gives away." Indeed, Luther noted that this is what goodness, the fruit of the Spirit, means.[15]

Luther offered many practical ways to cultivate generosity in our lives. In outlining the positive way to keep the Seventh Commandment in his *Personal Prayer Book*, Luther called on Christians "to be poor in spirit [Matt. 5:3], generous, willing to lend or give of our possessions, and to live free of avarice and covetousness." In the Large Catechism, he exhorted us to be cognizant of "how you deal with the poor—there are many of them now—who must live from hand to mouth." Further, he warned that those in positions of authority should "have the courage to establish and maintain order in all kinds of trade and commerce . . . lest the poor be burdened and oppressed."[16] Luther held love for our neighbor to be the guiding principle that should inform any decisions we make in the economic realm—a principle that should also cause us to push back against instances of injustice that exist in our world.[17]

A generous heart, Luther said, "is not concerned for its own sake, but for the neighbor's sake." It forgets its own interests, is not concerned with its own advantage or wealth, for "the man whose money is dear to him and who is on the lookout for his own advantage will not have much regard for his neighbor or for the office that involves his neighbor." Thus he concluded that "no greedy belly can be a Christian."[18]

The Seventh, Ninth, and Tenth Commandments call us to watch zealously over what belongs to our neighbor. A greedy heart hinders us from keeping this command, as we idolatrously cling to our possessions in an effort to secure our own good. But generosity toward others helps us kill our greed by forcing us to recognize that all our needs are supplied by God, not our own cunning. As our trust in God's provision grows, the Holy Spirit enables us to live generously for the sake of our neighbors.

REFLECTION QUESTIONS

1. Jesus says, "Where your treasure is, there will your heart be also" (Luke 12:34). Paul says that "the love of money is a root of all kinds of evil" (1 Timothy 6:10). What does this teach us about the nature of greed?

2. Read Matthew 6:24–26. How does Jesus' teaching here relate to the sin of greed and its potential consequences?

3. Read the parable of the rich fool in Luke 12:13–21. What does Jesus teach here about wealth and greed?

4. According to 1 Timothy 6:17–18, what attitude should Christians have toward money and earthly goods instead of greediness?

5. What instruction and encouragement does Hebrews 13:5–6 offer?

CHAPTER 9

KILLING GLUTTONY AND LUST:

TEMPERANCE/CHASTITY

The Sixth Commandment
You shall not commit adultery.

"It Feels So Right, It Can't Be Wrong . . ."

When it comes to issues of sexuality, gender, and marriage in our society, there is massive contention and even more confusion. For a conservative Christian, it might seem so simple: God created both men and women. Men and women come together in marriage, bring forth children, and the cycle repeats—this is how the world goes round and continues from generation to generation.

But today people argue about whether children should be allowed to surgically "change" their gender, about whether a man who identifies as a woman can use the women's restroom, about whether two women living together have a right to be "married" and enjoy the same kinds of societal recognition afforded to heterosexual unions. How did we get here? we might wonder. What's behind it all?

One answer is that our society is less moored to God's Word than generations prior and therefore less concerned with what Scripture says about sexuality. It would be hard to counter such an argument. But let's dig a bit deeper. Scripture reveals that the underlying cause of sexual confusion involves matters of the sinful heart.

Paul wrote to the church in Rome that men became "futile in their thinking" when they no longer acknowledged God's presence in the world and that their "foolish hearts" became darkened (1:20–22). In Romans 1:23–25, he diagnosed the problem as idolatry, prioritizing created things over the Creator. But as we've learned, idolatry takes a variety of forms. Which specific form of idolatry predominates when a society shuns knowledge of God altogether? Paul is clear: "God gave them up in the lusts of their hearts to impurity. . . . God gave them up to dishonorable passions" (Romans 1:24, 26). In short, one telltale symptom that a society no longer acknowledges the Creator God is when lustful passions are given free reign.

At the heart of our confusion over sexuality is the vice of lustful desire, which seeks physical pleasure by whatever means without consideration for God's will or the harm it does to our neighbor—if it makes me feel good, who is anyone else to tell me it's wrong? But the vice of lust isn't just in "society." Lust is a problem even within marriages that proceed according to God's design. The Sixth Commandment offers clarity amidst this confusion, instructing us on the parameters and purpose of marriage, showing how the vice of lust corrupts those good boundaries, and prompting us to pursue the virtues of chastity and temperance instead of sinful desire.

The Sixth Commandment—Marriage and Sexuality

In the Large Catechism, Luther noted that the commandments "show that we must avoid doing any kind of harm to our neighbor." The Sixth Commandment, with its prohibition against adultery, exists to protect our nearest neighbor—our spouse— and the boundaries of marriage in general. Luther understood that adultery is specifically forbidden because it was the most common form of unchastity, but he taught that the commandment "is directed against all kinds of unchastity, whatever it may be called."[1]

Luther summarized the good work that flows from this commandment in his explanation in the Small Catechism: We "fear and love God so that we lead a sexually pure and decent life in what we say and do, and husband and wife love and honor each other." You may notice something different about this explanation compared to others in the Small Catechism: it is the only commandment for which Luther does not list particular prohibitions. Because the Small Catechism was written to instruct young people, Luther wisely refrained from discussing how one might transgress this command—hence there is no mention of avoiding unchastity or lust. However, he included various prohibitions in his *Personal Prayer Book*, which was not written with children in mind.[2]

Luther also explained how the Sixth Commandment teaches us about the estate of marriage:

> **This commandment is aimed directly at the state of marriage. . . . God honors and praises this estate. . . . Therefore, He also wishes us to honor it. . . . He created man and woman separately, as is clear [Genesis 1:27]. This was not for lewdness, but so that they might live together in marriage, be fruitful, bear children, and nourish and train them to honor God. . . . Married life is, therefore, no joke or presumption. It is an excellent thing and a matter of divine seriousness. For marriage has the highest importance to God so that people are raised up who may serve the world and promote the knowledge of God, godly living, and all virtues.[3]**

Here we see how this commandment is ultimately designed to serve the good of our neighbor well beyond the home through the blessings of marriage.

Modern assumptions and perspectives about marriage and sexuality often go against God's design for His creatures. These pervasive beliefs can influence Christians, turning us from the truth of Scripture and eventually sabotaging our efforts to uphold the Sixth Commandment. Our understanding of romantic love in particular has affected how we view marriage. Western culture sees love primarily as a feeling rather than a commitment. This faulty understanding allows human passion to dominate our actions and relationships, resulting in affairs, living together before marriage, divorce, and so many other broken situations.

This brokenness certainly affects our own lives and the lives of anyone involved. For Christians, however, the consequences extend further. When followers of Jesus don't take His prescriptions for sexuality seriously, it undermines our witness and service to the rest of the world when we try to speak God's truth into other matters related to sexuality—issues such as same-sex relationships or gender fluidity. Scripture is clear about God's design for human sexuality: we are created as men and women (Genesis 1:27; Matthew 19:4), marriage is meant to be a lifetime bond between one man and one woman (Matthew 19:5-6), and sex is given for our benefit only within the committed relationship of marriage (Hebrews 13:4). How can we expect others to listen to our witness on such issues when our own lives do not reflect these truths?

We may think of these issues as unique to our time, but Scripture shows that humans have always struggled with sexual sin. Paul wrote to the Corinthians, for example, about many sexual issues affecting their faith and their witness to the surrounding culture. Luther, too, dealt with this type of issue. In his day, priests were not allowed to marry, which compelled them to celibacy. Luther considered such a marriage ban to be elevating human rules above what God had clearly ordained: God has created us as men and women, so we are not "given the power to make a woman out of a man or a man out of a woman, or to nullify either sex. . . . [Likewise we have] no authority to separate such creatures of God, or to forbid them from living honestly in marriage with one another," as the priests were forced to do. The Augsburg Confession further notes that "complaints about unchaste priests [were] common," again demonstrating the damage to ourselves, our neighbor, and our witness that occurs when we live apart from God's design.[4]

In all these cases, we attempt to re-create sexuality or marriage in our own image instead of reflecting what God has given to us. Whether it's prohibiting priests from marrying, having sex apart from a committed marriage, or attempting to live as a different gender, we damage ourselves and our neighbors when we twist marriage and sexuality to fit our wishes instead of God's commands. Through these applications, we clearly see how the Sixth Commandment informs our understanding of the true nature of marriage and extends to every aspect of our created sexuality.[▼]

▼ For a more complete treatment of the Sixth Commandment and its applications to our modern context, see the section on the Sixth Commandment in the 2017 edition of *Luther's Small Catechism with Explanation* from Concordia Publishing House (Questions 65–77).

Gluttony and Lust

Because men and women are created by God for each other, Luther strongly believed that they should ordinarily be found in the estate of marriage. He encouraged godly marriage for the blessings it brings to society, but he also knew marriage was necessary to help avoid unchastity. Thus, he applied the Sixth Commandment to everyone—married or unmarried—by showing how it prohibits all sexual immorality.[5] And the particular vices that lead us to unchastity are gluttony and lust.

Wait, you might be thinking, gluttony? While this might not be the most obvious pairing for a modern reader, the connection between unchastity and gluttony is clear from Scripture, Luther, and the ancient church fathers. Luther called gluttony and drunkenness "weapons of unchastity."[6] Paul expresses the same sentiment in Ephesians 5:18: "Do not get drunk on wine, for that is debauchery." Evagrius, too, taught that gluttony gives rise to lustful thoughts and actions and observed how food and drink fuel the fires of unchastity.[7]

Luther also linked gluttony and lust when considering the "desires of the flesh" from 1 John 2:16: "The lust of the flesh is that pleasure with which I desire to indulge my flesh, such as adultery, fornication, gluttony, ease, and sleep."[8] Gluttony and lust encourage unchastity because they teach us to give in to sinful desires. Thomas Aquinas defined gluttony as inordinate desire for food or drink.[9] In the vice tradition, more than just overeating, gluttony included eating or drinking too particularly, too expensively, too ravenously, or before the proper time. In other words, gluttony means we cannot manage our desires around food and drink.

Why is this important? As Gregory the Great observed, those who cannot control what they consume have not even begun to engage in the spiritual fight.[10] With gluttony, we train ourselves to feel "full" only by sating the stomach; we never learn what it means to live not "by bread alone, but by every word that comes from the mouth of God" (Matthew 4:4). As with greed, gluttony finds pleasure in the created things of the world instead of in the Creator. Rather than a good gift from God to sustain us, food becomes an idol, as Paul once pronounced: "Their end is their destruction; their god is their belly" (Philippians 3:19).

Controlling our gluttonous desires is training ground for the battle against stronger desires of the flesh. If we do not train ourselves to say no to a simple morsel of food, how can we control the urges and passions of sexual desire? Not surprisingly, then, fasting can help to kill passions of the flesh, such as gluttony and lustful intent. When our stomachs are always full, more important desires for enduring things are never permitted to emerge. But when we find ourselves most empty inside, most vulnerable, we come to understand what our deepest and most driving passions truly are and hence learn most to depend on God. This ultimately drives out unbelief and strengthens faith.

Luther understood that conquering gluttonous desire is essential to this fight: ▾

▾ For an extended treatment of gluttony, see Luther's 1539 "Sermon on Soberness and Moderation against Gluttony and Drunkenness," based on 1 Peter 4:7–11 (LW 51:290–99).

> Reveling and drunkenness foment unchastity. . . . Thus the holy fathers stated that he who wishes to serve God must above all fight against the vice of gluttony, because it is both the first and the most difficult vice to overcome. If this is not rooted out, even if it does not lead to . . . lasciviousness, . . . yet it renders the mind unprepared over against divine matters. For this reason fasting is one of the strongest weapons of Christians, but gluttony is one of the most potent machines of the devil.[11]

Lust has a more obvious connection to unchastity, but the principle behind it is the same as gluttony: indulging our desire for pleasure. As Jesus showed in Matthew 5:28, breaking the Sixth Commandment is more than the act of adultery; even a lustful glance is adultery of the heart. Not all sexual desire is sinful lust, of course. God created sex and sexual desire for His good purposes and our pleasure, which Luther's explanation of the Sixth Commandment pointed out, but lust distorts that gift.

The vice tradition distinguished two ways lust damages God's good gift of sex: (1) turning sexual pleasure into meaningless, base instinct or (2) elevating it as spiritual ecstasy to be pursued by any means. We degrade sex, even within Christian marriage, when we pursue it as personal gratification rather than an act that cherishes and nourishes our partner and the marriage relationship itself.

When we lust, we attempt to engineer our own happiness—another example of idolatry. We also sin against our partner, treating that person as a means to our own ends instead of a valuable end in his or her own right. Whether through adultery, pornography, or any other lustful desire, we are choosing a counterfeit version of the pleasure that God has designed us to experience in the one-flesh union of marriage.

The apostle Peter warns about the danger of giving in to these vices: "Beloved, I urge you . . . to abstain from the passions of the flesh, which wage war against your soul" (1 Peter 2:11). Our salvation is at stake when we let our unchaste desires control us, as with gluttony and lust. Concerning the fight against lust, Luther wrote:

> Those who say that they have faith . . . [but] live as they please . . . are deceiving themselves. Where faith is genuine, it must attack the body and hold it in check, lest the body do what it pleases. For this reason, St. Peter says that we must be sober [1 Peter 1:13].[12]

To hold our desires in check, we must attack gluttony and lust by cultivating their opposite virtue—chastity.

Chastity, Temperance, and Self-Control

Luther's explanation of the Sixth Commandment calls us to "lead a sexually pure and decent life in what we say and do." Older translations of the catechism rendered this as "a chaste and decent life." We don't often see the word *chaste* today, but the newer translation conveys its meaning well—sexual purity. The virtue of chastity battles against the sexual impurity fostered by lust and gluttony.

Consider Luther's description of the virtue: "Real chastity is the kind which does battle with impurity, struggles against it, and unceasingly drives out all the poison injected by the flesh and the devil." This is difficult, daily work. In fact, Luther said that "if no other work but chastity were commanded, we would have our hands full doing it" because our unchaste desires never cease. Drawing on Romans 13:12–14, Luther said that we must employ the "godly weapons" of "fasting, watching, and working" against these desires to master unchastity.[13]

To pursue chastity, then, means to exercise the classical virtue of temperance, or the fruit of the Spirit Paul called self-control. According to Luther,

> [The fruit of self-control] refers to sobriety, temperance, or moderation in every walk of life. Paul . . . wants Christians to live a chaste and sober life; not to be adulterers, immoral or lustful persons; . . . not to be drunken, not to be addicted to intoxication. . . . All this is included in chastity or self-control."[14]

By specifically equating this fruit of the Spirit with the cardinal virtue of temperance, Luther showed that the philosophical virtue tradition could align with Christian virtue when its reasoning aligned with Scripture. Luther wrote that self-control is "'temperance,' which we must understand in reference not only to chastity but also to drink and food. Its meaning, therefore, embraces chastity and moderation.'"[15] We must earnestly pursue the virtue of chastity to mortify the desires of the lustful flesh and carry out the work of living a sexually pure and decent life in all we say and do.

The Sixth Commandment applies to every facet of our created sexuality. By drawing the vice and virtue tradition into this commandment, Luther added more definition to its already rich contours. To order our lives according to God's design, we must kill the idols of lust and gluttony by developing temperance. Temperance shuns the passions of the flesh, be it food and drink or sexual pleasure, freeing the heart to instead find pleasure in serving God and our neighbor by our actions and example.

REFLECTION QUESTIONS

1. What act does the Sixth Commandment explicitly forbid? What does Jesus teach about the spirit of this commandment in Matthew 5:27–28?

2. Sexual sin was a significant problem in the Corinthian congregation. See what Paul writes to them in 1 Corinthians 6:12–20. How is sexual sin distinct from all other sin? According to Paul, how should Christians view their bodies differently than pagans do? What is his sole counsel for Christians who face sexual temptation?

3. Take a look at Colossians 3:5. What does Paul tell the Colossian Church to do with their impure desires? How might you do this in your own life? Consider creative ways to practice restraint toward sinful desire, such as fasting.

4. Why might it have been important for Jesus to fast before enduring Satan's temptations in the wilderness? (See Matthew 4:1–11.)

5. In place of lust and sexual immorality, the Bible encourages purity. Read 1 Corinthians 7:1–5 and Hebrews 13:4. What is Scripture's prescription for sexual desire? What does this teach us about God's plan for our sexuality?

CHAPTER 10

KILLING ANGER:

GENTLENESS, PATIENCE, AND FORGIVENESS

The Fifth Commandment
You shall not murder.

The Fourth Commandment
Honor your father and your mother.

God's Slow Nostrils

After four hundred years of slavery under Pharaoh, God's people were freed. God miraculously rescued them and set them on the path to the Promised Land. On their way, God brought them to Mount Sinai to give them the Ten Commandments—decrees to guide their life together in the new land. The number one command was to have no other gods.

While Moses was on the mountaintop receiving these commandments etched onto two stone tablets by the very finger of God, the Israelites down at the foot of the mountain grew restless. They feared Moses has died. They engaged in revelry. They melted down the gold from their plunder of the Egyptians, fashioned a statue in the form of a calf (a pagan deity popular with neighboring nations), and did the unthinkable: they bowed down and worshiped that golden calf, saying, "These are your gods, O Israel, who brought you up out of the land of Egypt!" (Exodus 32:4). Seeing this, God told Moses, "I have seen this people, and behold, it is a stiff-necked people. Now therefore let Me alone, that My wrath may burn hot against them and I may consume them" (Exodus 32:9–10).

But then something remarkable happened. Moses pleaded with God, for the sake of His promises, to turn aside from His burning anger and from destroying the Israelites. And God did. He relented and determined to stick with this wayward people and make of them a great nation, from which He would eventually bring a Savior. To symbolize that the Lord had not turned aside from the promises He made to His people, He commanded Moses to go back up the mountain and make another copy of the Ten Commandments—for Moses had broken the first set when he saw the Israelites worshiping an idol. As the Lord approached Moses, He then proclaimed the full reality of His name: "The LORD, the LORD, a God merciful and gracious, slow to anger, and abounding in steadfast love and faithfulness" (Exodus 34:6).

Slow to anger. Literally in Hebrew, it says God is "long in two nostrils." Huh? How do you get "slow to anger" from "long nostrils"? Well, it's not as big a mental leap as it appears. "Long" here refers to a length of time, as in "taking a long time," so it could also be rendered "slow" or perhaps even "patient." One visible sign of anger is flaring our nostrils. It's a telltale clue that someone is mad. If someone is long, or slow, in the nostrils, that means it takes a lot for them to get angry. And that's how God described Himself.

What causes your own nostrils to flare in anger? Is it circumstances you can't control? Maybe people who get on your nerves? Money? Events going on in the world around you? An opinion you disagree with? Whatever your triggers are, know that anger is more than an emotion. The vice of anger that wells up in our heart can undermine our efforts to live in accordance with God's will—particularly with His commands to not murder and to honor those who hold authority over us.

When we witness or experience injustice, our sinful nature wants to mete out justice or punishment in the present, by our own volition. In anger, we attempt to distribute our own wrath upon others in advance of God's proper judgment, exposing the reality that we do not trust God or His authorities to be just and avenge us. However, pursuing the virtues that oppose anger—peace, patience, and forgiveness—helps to form us into people who honor and uphold the lives and livelihoods of others.

The Fifth Commandment—Body and Life

The Fifth Commandment concerns our responsibility to uphold the physical well-being and lives of our neighbors. According to Luther,

> **Christ Himself explains and sums it up [in Matthew 5:20–26]. He says that we must not kill, neither with hand, heart, mouth, signs, gestures, help, nor counsel. Therefore, this commandment forbids everyone to be angry, except those . . . who are in the place of God, that is, parents and the government.[1]**

The words of our Lord in the Sermon on the Mount force us to recognize that "murder" extends to the heart, for "everyone who is angry with his brother will be liable to judgment; whoever insults his brother will be liable to the council; and whoever says, 'You fool!' will be liable to the hell of fire" (Matthew 5:22). Drawing on this to interpret the Fifth Commandment, church fathers such as Augustine and Aquinas said that the "origin and root of killing do not lie in our hand" but rather "lie in the heart overcome by anger."[2] Luther, too, recognized this progression:

[When we are angry with others,] our hearts also would like to rage and bleed and take vengeance. Then there arise cursing and blows. From them misery and murder finally come. . . . Where murder is forbidden, all cause from which murder may spring is also forbidden. For many people, although they do not kill, curse and utter a wish that would stop a person from running far if it were to strike him on the neck.[3]

Luther saw that the Fifth Commandment "also applies to anyone who can do his neighbor good, prevent or resist evil, defend, and save his neighbor so that no bodily harm or hurt happen to him—yet does not do this." While Christians might not physically harm a neighbor very often, we regularly break this commandment by sins of omission—by neglecting to "help and support [our neighbor] in every physical need," as the Small Catechism instructs.[4]

The Fifth Commandment also forces us to recognize that we are not in control of life and death. God is. Whether out of anger or a sense of justice or for any other reason, individual humans do not have authority to take life. That responsibility belongs only to God and His representatives. Contemporary society seems to attack life from beginning to end: through abortion, suicide, and euthanasia, for example. Christians trust God as the author of life, and we therefore relinquish our desire to control life and death to Him. The Fifth Commandment means that we must treasure and defend life, as God does, not snuff it out for our own purposes.

The Fourth Commandment—God's Representatives

We know that God has all authority over our lives. The Fourth Commandment helps us understand who God has appointed as His representatives over us in this life. "To the position of fatherhood and motherhood God has given special distinction above all positions that are beneath it," Luther said.[5] God places our parents over us as His representatives, giving them the responsibility to raise children in the faith and teach them godly virtues by which to serve our neighbor.

We are therefore called to honor our parents, to "serve and obey them, love and cherish them."[6] The opposite, of course, would be to dishonor them by despising and angering them. While this task can sometimes prove difficult, nevertheless we obey God when we honor our parents, recognizing the enormous responsibility they have.

Luther also expanded the application of the Fourth Commandment to include "all those who are set in authority over us." He gave particular attention to civil authorities because "through them, as through our parents, God gives to us food, house and home, protection, and security. . . . It is our duty to honor them and to value them greatly."[7] Luther often noted the many blessings God bestows through governmental authorities:

> God sustains government and through it gives
> peace and punishes and guards against the wicked,
> so that we may support wife and children, bring up
> children in the discipline and knowledge of God,

have security in our homes and on the streets, that each may help the other, and communicate and live with another. Such gifts are altogether heaven, and God desires that we consider and recognize them as gifts of God. He desires us to honor government as a servant of his and to show gratitude to it because through it God gives us such great benefits.[8]

Sometimes those who have been entrusted with these earthly responsibilities abuse their power. However, even when Christians are subject to a government they find displeasing or burdensome, we are still called to obedience. The office of these authorities remains divinely ordained, as Paul teaches in Romans 13:2: "Whoever resists the authorities resists what God has appointed, and those who resist will incur judgment."

Luther echoed this in various teachings about rebellion against authorities, which was an important issue in his day. He also pointed out that rebellion "never brings about the desired improvement. For insurrection lacks discernment; it generally harms the innocent more than the guilty. Hence, no insurrection is ever right, no matter how right the cause it seeks to promote."[9] As with the Fifth Commandment, we are called to trust that God is the ultimate authority over life and well-being and that He will make good on His promises to provide for us, just like He did for the Israelites.

Of course, Scripture acknowledges that there is a limit to the Christian's obedience to earthly authority. "We must obey God rather than men," Peter says (Acts 5:29). When a temporal ruler commands us to act contrary to God's will, the Christian must disobey. In these situations, Luther instructed Christians to say this:

> "It is not fitting that Lucifer should sit at the side of God. Gracious sir, I owe you obedience in body and property; command me within the limits of your authority on earth, and I will obey. But if you command me to believe or to get rid of certain books, I will not obey; for then you are a tyrant and overreach yourself, commanding where you have neither the right nor the authority," etc. Should he seize your property on account of this and punish such disobedience, then blessed are you; thank God that you are worthy to suffer for the sake of the divine word.[10]

When we must, out of allegiance to God, disobey earthly authorities, we will face the established consequences. However, we can bear the punishment with a spirit of joy, knowing that we suffer for the name of Christ and trusting God's greater authority (see 1 Peter 3:13–17; 4:12–19).

Anger

The Fourth and Fifth Commandments both teach us about God's authority over our lives and how we are to respond to that authority: by upholding our neighbor's life and well-being and by honoring those whom God has placed over us as His representatives. The vice of anger particularly affects our ability to protect others and honor authorities.

Anger has a complicated history among the capital vices. Unlike the others, it is not always blatant sin, as Paul implies in Ephesians 4:26: "Be angry and do not sin." Sometimes anger serves as a positive motivator, spurring us toward necessary action for the good of others. Luther once quipped to a friend: "I have no better remedy than anger. If I want to write, pray, preach well, then I must be angry. Then my entire blood supply refreshes itself, my mind is made keen, and all temptations depart."[11]

Jesus Himself expressed anger. Mark records an occasion when Jesus "looked around at them with anger, grieved at their hardness of heart" (3:5). All the Gospels include the account of Jesus upending the money-changers' tables in the temple, apparently due to anger He felt upon discovering that His Father's house had been turned into a "den of robbers" (e.g., Matthew 21:13).

We often call this a "righteous anger." While such anger is theoretically possible for humans, Scripture teaches that "the anger of man does not produce the righteousness of God" (James 1:20). Indeed, nearly every list of sins in the New Testament includes anger or its equivalent. In the best light, anger over wrongdoing would merely desire to restore justice, which is why Aquinas defined the vice of anger as the love of justice perverted into the desire for revenge. When we get angry too easily, get angry at the wrong entity, get more angry than we should, or remain angry for too long, for example, emotion has given way to vice, and outward manifestations of sin are rarely far behind.[12] Because anger gives "the devil a foothold," Christians should be "slow to anger," after the example of our Lord (Ephesians 4:27 NIV; James 1:19; Exodus 34:6).

Luther cautioned against "righteous anger," knowing how easy it is to confuse love of justice with misguided zeal:

> [Some] seek punishment to be meted out, not because they seek their own advantage, but through the punishment and restoration of their own things they seek the betterment of the one who has stolen or offended. . . . But no one ought to attempt this unless he is mature and highly experienced . . . lest he mistake wrath for zeal and be convicted of doing from anger and impatience that which he believes he is doing from love of justice.[13]

New Testament scholar Jeffrey Gibbs offers this wise counsel on how Christians should understand anger:

> The Bible, and especially the New Testament, teaches straightforwardly that human anger is a common and dangerous reality in our lives. That is the dominant message, and it should be the dominant way that Christians think about their anger. It would be going too far, I believe, to say that the emotional reaction of anger is always and intrinsically sinful; it is not. It would not be going too far, however, to say that anger is always spiritually

dangerous and that we need to deal with it seriously and piously. . . . The connection between anger and actual sin is so close that both Christ Jesus and his apostles can simply equate the two: anger in many New Testament texts simply is a form of sin. . . .

Nowhere [in Scripture] . . . are we commanded to act in righteous anger and even when it seems a possibility (as with Eph 4:25–27 or Jas 1:18–19), there is an immediate warning against sinning. . . . In the case of Moses or Elijah or Paul, the texts do narrate that they were angry and then acted in response to evil of some sort. But this does not mean we should think that our anger is like theirs, or even that in their anger they did not sin at all. And if someone would like to appeal to the anger of Almighty God or of the Lord Jesus Christ in support for the category of "righteous anger," the simple answer is that God is pure and unable to sin and the Lord Jesus Christ was perfect. And we are not.[14]

For sinful humans, the vice of anger ultimately comes down to idolatry: an attempt to take God's justice into our own hands, standing in His place as the judge and avenger of wrongs.

The Fourth Commandment provides one exception to this guidance. Luther wrote that the Fifth Commandment "forbids everyone to be angry, except those . . . who are in the place of God, that is parents and the government." For those whose God-given vocations require them to punish wrongdoing, Luther con-sidered it proper for them "to be angry, to rebuke, and to punish because of those very persons who transgress this and the other commandments." Therefore, "God and the government are not included in [the prohibition on murder]. Nor is the power to kill taken away, which God and the government have."[15] Insofar as these representatives serve as agents of God and carry out His justice, they are authorized to bear the sword and potentially take life (see Romans 13:1–7).

Thus, Christians can with a clear conscience occupy secular positions that are required to take life, such as being soldiers.[16] In fact, Luther wrote that it

> would be quite un-Christian to say that there is any service of God in which a Christian should not or must not take part, when service of God is actually more characteristic of Christians than of anyone else. . . . For the sword and authority, as a partic-ular service of God, belong more appropriately to Christians than to any other men on earth.[17]

While God's earthly representatives have been granted this unique authority, Scripture also reminds us that Christians are not to return evil for evil but rather to "overcome evil with good" (Romans 12:21). For example, after Paul discusses the nature of the government's retributive work in Romans 13, he immediately turns our attention back to our personal callings, admonishing the individual Christian to "owe no one anything, except to love each other" (Romans 13:8).

Thus, Christians are called "to strive for meekness and to drive out anger"—to foster the virtues of peace, patience, gentleness, and forgiveness.[18]

Gentleness, Patience, and Forgiveness

We keep the Fifth Commandment by first recognizing that "God wants to remove the root and source by which the heart is embittered against our neighbor. . . . We learn to calm our wrath and to have a patient, gentle heart, especially toward those who give us cause to be angry."[19] Luther finished his explanation of the Fifth Commandment by pointing us to the fruit of the Spirit as a remedy for anger:

> Here again we have God's Word, by which He would encourage and teach us to do true, noble, and grand works such as *gentleness*, *patience*, and, in short, *love* and *kindness* to our enemies. . . . He is our God, which means He will help, assist, and protect us in order that He may quench the desire of revenge in us.[20]

We can trust that God will act justly to right any wrongs we face. We need not—and must not—take matters into our own hands to avenge wrongs, except as authorized by our God-given vocations. Sometimes authorities do not prosecute wrongs we have endured. Yet Christians practice patience continually, trusting God to act through His chosen means and at His preferred time. Luther encouraged us to remember that "even if government cannot in every instance punish [wrongdoing,] . . . still we should know that God will punish."[21] The Lord claims vengeance for Himself (Romans 12:19) and will eventually bring His justice to bear, whether now or on the Last Day.

Instead, we treat others with gentleness, patience, and love. The fruit of gentleness is a "virtue by which one is not easily provoked to anger. Innumerable occasions in this life provoke us to anger, but they are conquered by gentleness." Christians exemplify these virtues when they are "not quarrelsome and do not hate one another but bear one another's burdens . . . with patience; for without patience peace cannot continue." When a Christian "not only bears adversity, insults, injury, etc., but even waits patiently for some improvement in those who have harmed him," we serve our neighbor and uphold the Fourth and Fifth Commandments.[22]

Finally, Christians also battle anger with the gift of forgiveness. Forgiveness is essential to quelling anger. We are called to extend the same forgiveness to our neighbor that our Lord has provided for us, as we pray in the Lord's Prayer: "Forgive us our trespasses, as we forgive those who trespass against us." It is difficult to remain angry with someone whom we genuinely forgive. Luther warned, however, that to withhold forgiveness from another in anger is to risk eternal consequences:

> What harm has [your enemy] done you? Simply a temporal harm. Why would you, because of this trivial, temporal hurt, bring eternal harm to yourself? Beware O man! Not he who offends you but

you who refuse to forgive inflicts a harm on you greater than the whole world could do.[23]

Anger, like the other vices that arise in our hearts, must be killed. The Fourth and Fifth Commandments call followers of Jesus to foster a patient, gentle, and forgiving heart—one that is willing to bear wrongs, a heart that responds not with anger but with trust in God and respect for those in authority. In this way, we honor God's authority and protect our neighbors from harm.

REFLECTION QUESTIONS

1. How does Jesus interpret the Fifth Commandment in Matthew 5:21–22?

2. Read Ephesians 4:26–27. What is the danger of allowing anger to linger in our life?

3. What does Paul instruct in Colossians 3:8 regarding anger? In verses 12–13, Paul tells us what should replace anger in our life. What qualities will Christians display instead? Why is forgiveness particularly important?

4. Read Romans 12:14–21. How should Christians respond to those who might cause them to be angry? Whose job is it to avenge evil in our world?

CHAPTER 11

KILLING SLOTH:

DILIGENCE/ZEAL

The Third Commandment
Remember the Sabbath day by keeping it holy.

Keeping God's Day Holy

Beep beep beep. Beep beep beep.

You pull your head slightly off the pillow, peek through one squinted eye at the fuzzy red numerals of the alarm clock, and somehow make contact with the snooze button. Seemingly seconds later, the blaring noise sounds again. You know you need to get up now if you want to make it to church on time.

But it's been a long week, you think. The kids are exhausted. They've been up too late. You've got your nephew's birthday party later in the day, and if the kids are tired and cranky, it's not going to be pretty. You've got a list of chores that still needs to be done before the weekend is through. If you had an extra hour or two this morning to get some of those done, you'd feel much better heading into the week ahead. You sigh. We went to church a couple of weeks ago, I think, you assure yourself. Missing again won't hurt near as bad as having everyone start their week off out of sync. Besides, God knows we need our rest—that's what the Sabbath is all about, right?

And with that, you turn the alarm off completely. Something tugs at your conscience, but the feeling doesn't last long, because soon you are fast asleep once again—and this is slothful indeed.

We don't often hear the word *sloth* anymore. Ask a kid what "sloth" is, and they'll probably tell you it's an animal that moves very, very slowly. We hear about laziness more frequently, likely picturing people who lay around a lot or don't work too hard at their jobs. And while we recognize that "lazy" is not the most flattering description, few would probably consider it a sin. You might be asking, What's wrong with taking it easy every now and then? It's true, there's nothing wrong with taking time off from the hustle and bustle of life. In fact, it's healthy for us to do so.

But the vice of sloth is not just "taking a break." More than physical lethargy, sloth describes our indifference toward the tasks to which God's Word calls us. Luther explicitly tied sloth to the Third Commandment and its command to keep our days holy by attending to God's Word.

The Third Commandment—Rest in God's Word

The Third Commandment applies differently to Christians than it did to the Old Testament Israelites. The New Testament teaches that, since the coming of Christ, our Sabbath rest is now a rest in Christ (see Hebrews 4:1–11). While the spiritual meaning of the command retains continuity across the Testaments, the immediate meaning as it applied to ancient Israel no longer concerns Christians.[1] Rather than following specific laws about work and rest as a way to keep the Sabbath holy, Luther explained that Christians sanctify, or make our days holy, through the Word of God: "We should fear and love God so that we do not despise preaching and His Word, but hold it sacred and gladly hear and learn it."[2]

The aspect of rest, however, is not completely eliminated. Nature and experience teach us that our bodies need rest so that we can be refreshed, so Luther recognized the necessity of refraining from work one day each week. But the primary intent is not to "stop working and be idle." Rather, this day allows us the "freedom and time to attend divine service . . . [and] come together to hear and use God's Word, and then to praise God, to sing and to pray." For Luther, the key aspect of the Third Commandment is the exhortation to "keep it holy" (Exodus 20:8; Deuteronomy 5:12). What does it mean to keep it holy? "Nothing else than to be occupied with holy words, works, and life." The day is already holy in and of itself, since it is created by God, but it becomes holy for us only when we "occupy ourselves with God's Word and exercise ourselves in the Word."[3]

Because "God's Word is the true 'holy thing' . . . [and] the treasure that sanctifies everything," Luther focused particularly on the Word—"taught, preached, heard, read, or meditated upon"—as the means to sanctify our days.[4]

Sloth

The command to keep the Sabbath holy involves active participation and attentiveness to the Word of God, the "one thing . . . necessary" (Luke 10:42). Therefore, Luther particularly noted sloth (or in Latin, *acedia*) as the vice that hinders our keeping of this commandment:

> God . . . will require of you an accounting of how you have heard, learned, and honored his Word. In the same way those conceited spirits should also be punished who, after they have heard a sermon

BATTLE *OF THE* **SOUL**

or two, become sick and tired of it and feel that
they know it all and need no more instructors.
This is precisely the sin that used to be numbered
among the mortal sins and was called [*acedia*]—
that is, laziness or weariness—a malignant, pernicious plague with which the devil bewitches and
deceives many hearts so that he may take us by
surprise and stealthily take the Word of God away
again.[5]

Late in his life, Luther opined that idleness is one of the greatest temptations:

The greatest temptation in the world is that nobody
fulfills his calling faithfully but everybody wishes
to indulge in idleness. I am now exhausted and full
of cares, yet I am plagued with many duties. Others
are idle and unwilling to do anything. I think that
if we didn't have to do what we do, if we weren't
driven to it, we wouldn't do anything either.[6]

The vice of sloth, following the pattern of all vice, then manifests itself in specific sins, especially sins of spurning the tasks
God's Word calls us to do—namely, to love God and to love our
neighbor as ourselves. Those bogged down by the vice of sloth
display apathy toward most every facet of daily life. "It is the sin
that believes in nothing, cares for nothing, seeks to know nothing, interferes with nothing, enjoys nothing, loves nothing, hates

nothing, finds purpose in nothing, lives for nothing, and only remains alive because there is nothing it would die for," as one writer put it.[7]

This is why Luther said that sloth is present in every commandment. Every command of God sets a duty before us, and if we consistently fail to love our neighbor through these duties, we are guilty of sloth. Faithful Christian living is not opposed to hard work; rather we are expected to "work with [our] hands," as Paul admonished (1 Thessalonians 4:11). Luther also made this point:

> **God wants to arouse the hearts of the saints so that they do not become smug and dull and perish from *acedia* ("from indifference") and from sluggishness of spirit. For if the spirit is aroused, faith is sharpened, the knowledge of God grows, and the new man is renewed from day to day and is taught what is the good and perfect will of God (cf. Rom. 12:2).[8]**

Sloth includes more than inaction. In the vice tradition, sloth also entailed spending too much time working on things that are not important. Some individuals busy themselves with various tasks at the expense of more important tasks, such as serving a neighbor or attending to God's Word. This, too, is slothful. As such, sloth is best understood as neglecting to engage in the good works God has called us to—whether our indifference springs from apathy or from wasting our time pursuing other, less important endeavors.

Luther warned of the danger of sloth and pointed to the only sure remedy:

> Since we are in the midst of enemies and are continually attracted by innumerable allurements, hindered by cares, and engaged in business affairs, through all of which we are withdrawn from purity of heart, therefore there is only one thing left for us: we must exhort ourselves with all zeal and, so to speak, stir up our sluggish spirit by means of the Word of God, by meditating on it, reading it, and continually listening to it. . . . If this did not happen, we would certainly be swallowed up in the end by the great number of those things, and *acedia* and *lukewarmness of spirit*, the greatest of all dangers, would overwhelm us. . . . For just as the body cannot do without its bread—otherwise it is weakened—so the heart of man is not strengthened except by this bread of God's Word. For as often as we forget the Word of God, so often do we fall back into the love of things and are polluted. We are cleansed from this pollution only when we return to the Word.[9]

Intentional engagement with and contemplation of the Word of God strengthens us against apathy and reminds us of our duty to our neighbor.

Because of the ever-present temptation to be slothful, Luther exhorted Christians to embrace their routine work for daily bread with zeal and trust in God: "Our toil must be motivated more by our desire to serve God through it, to avoid idleness, and to fulfill God's command addressed to Adam, 'In the sweat of your face you shall eat bread' [Gen. 3:19], rather than by our worrying and fretting over our nourishment. God will surely take care of this as long as we do our work according to his commandments." Thus, Luther prayed, "Grant that we may bear patiently and overcome whatever we must suffer [on account of God's kingdom] . . . , so that our poor flesh may not yield or fall away through weakness or sloth."[10]

Diligence and Zeal

Set in opposition to the vice of sloth is the virtue of diligence, which comes from the Latin *diligere*, meaning "to love." Diligence involves a sense of responsibility, dedication, and hard work that is committed to doing one's duties. For Christians, this includes a zeal for loving others. In fact, *zeal* is another name for the virtue contrary to sloth.

In commentary on Psalm 101, Luther extolled diligence and emphasized what it entails:

> David says here: "I am concerned about what is mine and look after those who are about me. Other kings should also be that solicitous about their own, so that if I venture to be too shrewdly and

busily occupied among strangers, I may not meanwhile neglect myself and those who are mine." And David may well be thankful for such a virtue. For it is indeed a very lovely thing and a special gift of God to be a good, *diligent* man who carefully looks after his own things and really pays serious attention to them, *especially to God's Word*, without letting extraneous matters lead him astray. Obedience is the crown and glory of all virtues; but if slothfulness is mingled with it, then . . . people become nothing but quacks, bunglers, and busybodies, who neglect much and cannot do anything for anyone out of love or gratitude.[11]

For Luther, our diligent determination to serve those around us depends on our attentiveness to God's Word, which calls each of us to our work.

Indeed, the reformer links faith and diligence together, instructing Christians:

Let him who wants to be holy and full of good works begin to exercise himself at all times in this faith in all his life and works. . . . Then he will find how much work he has to do, and how completely all things are included in faith, and how he may never grow idle because his very idling must be the exercise and work of faith.[12]

We exercise the virtue of diligence, then, in every good work God has commanded us to do, especially in learning the teachings of the church. As Luther concluded his discussion of the Third Commandment in the Large Catechism, he earnestly encouraged diligence in learning Scripture and the catechism:

> You are daily in the devil's kingdom. . . . He ceases neither day nor night to sneak up on you and to kindle in your heart unbelief and wicked thoughts against . . . the commandments. Therefore, you must always have God's Word in your heart, upon your lips, and in your ears. But where the heart is idle and the Word does not make a sound, the devil breaks in and has done the damage before we are aware. . . . On the other hand, the Word is so effective that whenever it is seriously contemplated, heard, and used, it is bound never to be without fruit. . . . It always awakens new understanding, pleasure, and devoutness and produces a pure heart and pure thoughts. . . . For these words are not lazy or dead, but are creative, living words.[13]

Sloth resists the difficult work of killing our sinful self and living out the virtuous habits of our new identity given in Christ. Jesus, however, invites us to zealously take up this task and promises that all who are weary and heavy laden can find their rest in Him, for as He teaches: "My yoke is easy, and My burden is light" (Matthew 11:30). By contrast, stubborn resistance to the transformation the Spirit attempts to work in our hearts is no easy burden to bear. The weight of guilt for works we have spurned through our sloth piles up and crushes us. The yoke of following Jesus and His demands is much lighter than the yoke of sloth we place upon ourselves when we refuse to take up our cross and obediently follow.

As Luther demonstrated, the Third Commandment highlights our need to attend to the Word of God and drink deeply from its well—learning its tenets and diligently living them out in our daily lives. Slothful indifference to God's commands impedes us from that daily work. As we grow in diligence and increasingly overcome our sluggish dispositions, we learn to hold God's Word sacred in our lives, and, upon hearing and learning it, we are freed to serve our neighbors with joyful zeal.

REFLECTION QUESTIONS

1. The book of Proverbs has a lot to say about the vice of sloth. Read Proverbs 6:6–11; 10:4; 12:27; 26:15; and 31:27. How do these passages portray sloth?

2. Read 2 Thessalonians 3:6–11. What does Paul warn against? What can idleness lead to?

3. Read 1 Thessalonians 5:14. How can serving others combat the vice of sloth?

4. Read the story of Mary and Martha in Luke 10:38–42. What does Jesus here teach is the one thing necessary in our lives to which we must continually attend? How can you prioritize studying God's Word in your life?

CHAPTER 12

KILLING PRIDE:
HUMILITY

The Second Commandment
You shall not misuse the name
of the Lord your God.

The First Commandment
You shall have no other gods.

Aristotle or Jesus?

When Aristotle first articulated the concept of virtue ethics, he produced a list of virtues and corresponding vices based on human reason and his perception of observed realities. In other words, it was based completely on natural revelation. Fallen human beings indeed possess a lingering understanding of what God's own goodness looks like based on the natural law written on our hearts (Romans 2:15). However, because this understanding is polluted by the sinful nature, we require special revelation to complete our picture of goodness as God defines it.

Christians recognize that God has provided that further revelation in Scripture and in Christ, whom the Scriptures proclaim. Thus, a specifically Christian ethic will differ from any ethic based on natural law alone, and the accompanying list of distinctly Christian virtues subsequently will also differ. Luther agreed, saying that "the virtues of the heathen must be distinguished from the virtues of Christians," but cautioned that "these distinctions require careful judgment."[1]

Luther employed that careful judgment as he reformed the vice and virtue tradition for use in the baptized Christian's daily battle against sin. Scripture reveals what natural revelation misses about virtue: its ultimate end is not improvement of self but service to the other. Thus, Luther moved away from the traditional philosophical virtues, which are prone to focus on self, and moved toward the fruit of the Spirit—virtues that have as their end service to our neighbor. In doing so, one trait in particular was turned on its head: pride.

Most philosophers considered pride a virtue—a sense of satisfaction in our own effort and accomplishment. But here is where a Christian understanding of virtue must differ, for Scripture shows that humility, rather than pride, is the central virtue necessary for keeping faith in God and serving our neighbor in love. In Jesus, in His life and teachings, we learn there is no greater virtue than humility.

The First and Second Commandments—Trust in the True God

The First Commandment calls Christians to "fear, love, and trust" exclusively in the one true God for our every need and blessing, as the Small Catechism explains. When we place our trust in created things or other creatures, we make them into idols and break the First Commandment.

The Second Commandment, with its call to honor God's name, is also concerned with where we place our hope and trust. We typically focus on avoiding the various ways we might misuse God's name "so that we do not curse, swear, use satanic arts, lie, or deceive by His name," as Luther explained in the Small Catechism. But we often overlook the positive aspect of keeping this command: calling upon God's name in our every trouble. Crying out to God in our need is perhaps the greatest way we honor His name. Using God's name in this manner bears witness that we are placing our ultimate trust in God and seeking help in Him alone.

More often, though, we seek help in other places or even in ourselves. What keeps us from placing our trust in God alone? In a word, pride—pride that stems from fear, that doubts God's power and goodness and says, "I must secure my own good." Indeed, every other vice is rooted in pride: Anger steps into God's spot as the judge and avenger of injustice. Envy steps into God's place in an attempt to be a more equitable distributor of worldly status. Sloth perpetually spurns the good works to which God calls us. Greed pridefully seeks security by attempting to possess far more than is necessary to sustain us. Lust and gluttony abuse the good gifts of God's creation, seeking fulfillment in self-created pleasure rather than in Christ.

Only by remaining in our place as creatures, receptive to the Creator's blessings, can we truly battle and, by God's grace, finally kill our pride.

Pride

Like his forebearers in the vice tradition, Luther understood pride to be the deadliest of all vices and further exposed pride as unbelief. Pride doubts God's goodness and refuses to trust in Him alone. Pride, Luther wrote, is a vice "contrary to these first two commandments," "an exceedingly dangerous sin, yet most common of all," and thus we should "flee from . . . and avoid all temporal honor and praise, and never . . . seek a name for oneself."[2]

Luther also knew that pride is often "the very last vice to be overcome" for several reasons. Luther drew on Augustine for the first reason, which is that pride does not always appear evil. Other vices are more obvious; they "are practiced in doing evil works."

But prideful "honor and self-satisfaction . . . are practiced in good works and by means of them."[3] Too often, pride hides beneath the veneer of what otherwise appear to be good works.

The second reason is that we are blind to our pride. Luther wrote:

> No one is certain that he is not continually committing mortal sin, because of the most secret vice of pride. . . . St. Gregory writes at the end of his *Moralia*, "How can we ever be saved, when our evil works are absolutely evil and our good works never absolutely good?" Again, Job 9[:21] says, "Though I were godly, even this my soul does not know," and again, "I am afraid in all my works, for I know thou dost not spare the sinner" [Job 9:28]. Commenting on this, St. Gregory says, "What I have done openly, I see; but what I have suffered secretly, I do not know." This means that no one can fully know his secret pride, . . . and through it all works are made unclean and cannot stand in the light of God's just judgment. This is what David says in Ps. 19[:12], "Lord, who can discern his errors? Clear thou me from hidden sins."[4]

When we are confronted about other vices present in our lives, we may make excuses for them or even deny them, but rarely will we defend them. Pride, however, turns our focus completely inward. We lack the objectivity to honestly assess our behavior.

And as Augustine recognized, it is far easier to fool ourselves because we take pride in "good" behaviors.

Finally, we struggle to overcome pride because "the world regards this terrible vice as the highest virtue." The world "always seeks things that are high . . . [and] wants to be exalted," but followers of Jesus are called to do the opposite; a Christian should "not want to exalt himself but should be content with what he has."[5] Luther's insight marks the difference between worldly virtue and virtue grounded in the commandments and teachings of Christ. The witness of the life of Christ leads to a dramatically different evaluation of pride.

Through Scripture, Luther understood and articulated what natural law could never tell us: pride is no virtue but rather the worst vice.

Humility

Over and against the vice of pride, the virtue of humility helps us position ourselves properly before the Lord. Humility is not self-deprecation, as it is commonly misunderstood. Rather, humility means to recognize that we are creatures, not the Creator. We were created from dirt (*humus* in Latin, hence humility) and have life only because God has breathed life into us. We are dependent on Him for every good thing. When we humbly embrace our role as His creatures, we overcome our pride, thereby allowing us to accomplish what Luther calls the "chief work" of faith: fearing, loving, and trusting in God above all things.[6]

Luther also understood humility as the virtue that opposes pride because it most exemplifies the pattern of Christ. He invoked Paul's words from Philippians 2:5–9 to make his case, emphasizing that Christ did not count His equality with God as something to hold on to "but rather desired to become our servant."[7] Luther continually returned to Paul's letter to support this insight, often paraphrasing Philippians 2:1–4:

> "Do nothing from selfishness or conceit, but in humility count others better than yourselves. Let each of you look not only to his own interests, but also to the interests of others." . . . Here we see clearly that the Apostle has prescribed this rule for the life of Christians, namely, that we should devote all our works to the welfare of others, since each has such abundant riches in his faith that all his other works and his whole life are a surplus with which he can by voluntary benevolence serve and do good to his neighbor.[8]

When Luther told Christians to follow the example of Christ, he had in mind Paul's description of Him in Philippians 2:1–11. By developing the servant mindset of Christ, our attitudes are transformed to be like His, so that our lives are oriented toward service to others.[9] Thus the virtue of humility addresses both our internal disposition and our actions. Luther held up Christ and His humility as the quintessential example for Christians of humble service:

So a Christian, like Christ his head, is filled and made rich by faith and should be content with this form of God which he has obtained by faith. . . . For this faith is his life, his righteousness, and his salvation: it saves him and makes him acceptable, and bestows upon him all things that are Christ's, as has been said above, and as Paul asserts in Gal. 2[:20] when he says, "And the life I now live in the flesh I live by faith in the Son of God." Although the Christian is thus free from all works, he ought in this liberty to empty himself, take upon himself the form of a servant, be made in the likeness of men, be found in human form, and to serve.[10]

We embrace virtue, not to create character for the sake of self-improvement or to puff up our pride and most certainly not to save ourselves but rather to be conformed to Christ for the sake of serving others. In Christlike humility, we daily battle the flesh and all sinful vice in the fight of faith.

REFLECTION QUESTIONS

1. Read the account of the fall of man in Genesis 3:1–7. How was humanity's fall related to the sin of pride? (See verse 5.)

2. In Matthew 6:1–4, Jesus specifically warns against pride in works. What does He say our attitude should be toward our good deeds? When are you most tempted to look pridefully on your works?

3. Read James 4:6–10. What is God's attitude toward the proud? What does He do for the humble? What is the eventual fate of those who humble themselves?

4. Read Philippians 2:3–11. How does Jesus' life follow the pattern of humility and subsequent exaltation? As Christians, how does this inform our interactions with others?

CONCLUSION

DRESSING FOR BATTLE
THE DAILY GARMENT OF BAPTISM

What Will You Wear Today?

When I teach on Baptism during confirmation class, I remind students that their status as baptized children of God should make a difference in how they live, and I encourage them to devise a way to remember their Baptism each morning as they begin their day. This can be something as simple as making a sign of the cross and saying, "In the name of the Father, Son, and Holy Spirit," at the end of a morning prayer.

I also point out that, since many of us start our day with a shower, that is another opportunity to remember our Baptism. As water hits our faces, we can recall that we were once touched by the waters of Holy Baptism and be reminded to allow this reality to impact how we live out the ensuing day.

The Scriptures in one place describe Baptism as a "washing of regeneration" (Titus 3:5), but otherwise they don't use any bathing or shower analogies as a means to remember our Baptism. However, they do employ another regular morning habit. Paul says that those who have been baptized in Christ have "put on" or clothed themselves with Christ (Galatians 3:27). Elsewhere, he writes to Christians and encourages them each day to "put on" such virtues as compassion, "kindness, humility, meekness, and patience"; to forgive one another; and to "put on love" (Colossians 3:12–14).

Paul also says that the "old self" and its practices must be "put off" (Colossians 3:9). Because the old man within us also wakes up each day, vying for our allegiance alongside the new man, Christians exercise a very real choice each day. The question remains for every believer: How will you dress? Will we wear the old rags of the sinful nature, dressing ourselves in deeds of darkness and depravity—will we wear our vices on our sleeve? Or will we put on our Baptism? Will we allow ourselves to be dressed with the spiritual virtues of love, joy, peace, patience, kindness, and the like?

In the Large Catechism, Luther encouraged all Christians to "regard their baptism as the *daily garment* that they are to wear all the time. Every day they should be found in faith and with its fruits, suppressing the old creature and growing up in the new."[1] Our Baptism should be like a piece of clothing we put on each day to remind ourselves that we are called to live differently from the rest of the world, to think and act differently, as those set apart for service to God's kingdom. Our baptismal garment is the battle-dress we don every day as we valiantly wage the battle of the soul.

Holy Habits

What does wearing our baptismal identity look like? Luther said, "If we want to be Christians, we must practice the work that makes us Christians."[2] We wear our Baptism each day by practicing holy habits that shape us into the people God intends to make of us.

Paul exhorts, "What you have learned and received and heard and seen in me—*practice these things*" (Philippians 4:9, emphasis added). The Lutheran Confessions remind us that, even though justified Christians have been liberated from the curse of the Law, nevertheless "they should *daily exercise* themselves in the Law of the Lord." We find in the Law "a mirror in which God's will and what pleases Him are exactly portrayed. This mirror should be *constantly held up to the believers and be diligently encouraged* for them without ceasing."[3]

It is certainly possible for a focus on developing virtue to contribute to a works-righteousness understanding of faith and detract from the central Reformation tenet of salvation by faith alone, as has been shown. But it is also a danger to believe that God's Law has no continuing place in our lives after we come to faith. The early reformers reminded God's people of the importance of practicing good works:

> For particularly in these last times it is no less necessary to admonish the people to Christian discipline and good works and to remind them how necessary it is that they practice good works as a demonstration of their faith and their gratitude to God than it is to admonish them that works not be mingled with the article on justification. For people can be damned by an Epicurean delusion about faith [i.e., that we can live however we want, without regard to God's commands] just as much as by the papistic, Pharisaic trust in their own works and merit.[4]

Aristotle called the development of virtue through repeated practice *habituation*. While Luther did not use this specific terminology, he nevertheless understood the importance of intentionally forming our lives in Christian virtue. He pointed out that Christians, especially young ones, must be trained in such a way that Christian truth "take root" in the heart. He said that the Christian should learn the Ten Commandments and "make them his daily exercise in all cases . . . as though they were written in every place wherever he would look, indeed wherever he walks or stands" and that we should "be occupied with the practice of this work for the rest of [our] life."[5]

Habituation is encouraged frequently in the Large Catechism, where Luther admonished each father "to question and examine his children and servants at least once a week and see what they know or are learning from the catechism. And if they do not know the catechism, he should keep them learning it faithfully." He endorsed training that shapes youth "in a childlike way and playfully in the fear and honor of God" so the commandments "might be kept well and in constant practice."[6]

Luther offered pragmatic counsel to those struggling with the vice of anger:

> Let him set his enemy before him, keeping him constantly before the eyes of his heart as an exercise whereby he may curb his spirit and accustom his heart to think kindly of his enemy, wish him all the best, care for him, and pray for him; and later, when the opportunity occurs, speak well of him and do good to him. Let him who is willing try

this, and if he does not find plenty to do as long as he lives, then let him make me a liar and say that what I said was wrong.[7]

Testing the heart for anger, purposeful prayer, encouraging words, and acts of kindness—Luther identified these as habits to be developed over a lifetime of intentional practice.

Whether it's dribbling a basketball or building a house, we must practice any given task in order to improve. Likewise, Christians are not immediately infused with every skill we might need to fight off temptation or to love our neighbor. We must expend regular and purposeful effort to become more godly people. Luther encouraged the faithful to "live right and straightforward and use all the blessings that God gives, just as a shoemaker uses his needle, awl, and thread for work."[8] Luther clearly understood that we acquire the skills necessary to live as Christians only through daily discipline. As a cobbler becomes more skilled in his craft from a lifetime of practice, so, too, we make use of our gifts and continually fine-tune our skill for living out the Christian life.

Christians can incorporate habituation without sacrificing the central tenet of Reformation theology, that of salvation apart from human performance. We develop virtue as part of the lifelong process of sanctification. This process, Luther said, is the meaning of our Baptism: that "the Old Adam in us should by daily contrition and repentance be drowned and die with all sins and evil desires, and that a new man should daily emerge and arise to live before God in righteousness and purity forever."[9] Being saved by faith alone is our beginning, but it is certainly not the end of the Christian life. Christ's saving work sets us along the path of becoming more holy.

Luther recommended two habits in particular to help Christians on this path: confession and prayer. These habits encourage us to move away from vice and toward virtue, readying us to carry out God's holy commands in service to our neighbors.

Confessing Our Vices

The first habit Luther suggested is to confess our vices—that is, to regularly examine our conscience in light of the vices at work within our heart. He counseled:

> Proceed to the Second Table of the commandments. See how disobedient you have been and are still toward father and mother and all in authority; how you sin against your neighbor with *anger*, . . . how you are tempted to *unchastity, covetousness*, and injustice . . . against your neighbor.[10]

In a guiding document that Luther and his colleague Philip Melanchthon crafted for use in visiting and assessing the spiritual health of area churches, they encouraged preachers to point out and condemn specific vices present in the lives of the faithful:

> Proclaim and explain the Ten Commandments often and earnestly. . . . Point out and condemn various specific vices, as adultery, drunkenness,

envy, and hate, and how God has punished these, indicating that without doubt after this life he will punish still more severely if there is not improvement here.[11]

In encouraging this practice, Luther returned a theology of vice to one of its original purposes. That was one way the monastic fathers used the classification of the deadly sins. The vices help us diagnose which sins are present in our heart, allowing our confession to be specific to our unique struggles as sinners. When we can properly name the particular sins that plague us, we are better equipped to battle them.

This insight from Luther and the early church provides impetus for the church today to supplement her own practice of confession. A common confession found in *Lutheran Service Book* reads:

Most merciful God, we confess that we are by nature sinful and unclean. We have sinned against You in thought, word, and deed, by what we have done and by what we have left undone. We have not loved You with our whole heart; we have not loved our neighbors as ourselves. We justly deserve Your present and eternal punishment. For the sake of Your Son, Jesus Christ, have mercy on us. Forgive us, renew us, and lead us, so that we may delight in Your will and walk in Your ways to the glory of Your holy name. Amen.[12]

This confession is rooted in the language of Scripture and helps Christians express that they have not loved as Christ has called them to. However, while it confesses sins of "*thought*, word, and deed," the generic language of "failure to love" does not consider specifically which kinds of thoughts, inner desires, and passions have specifically transgressed God's will. The implied prescription moving forward then is simply a renewed call to love God and others. But how?

Confessing in the language of vice provides more specificity, helping to fine-tune our confession so we can identify and target how our efforts to love might more consistently reflect God's holy will—specific ways to "delight in [God's] will and walk in [His] ways." For example, if I struggle with greed, I can grow in generosity. If I struggle with anger, I can practice patience. So, in our confession, perhaps believers could be intentional about more regularly examining ourselves for which vices have a grip on our heart. To help with this task, I have created a prayer of confession, found in the "Prayers" section at the end of this book, that uses the language of vice in Scripture.

The Small Catechism displays this sort of specificity in the section on confession. It instructs us to "consider [our] place in life according to the Ten Commandments" and to ask ourselves whether we have been "lazy" (slothful), "hot-tempered" (angry), and more. Most of the list involves confession of outward deeds, such as being "quarrelsome" or stealing, but the language does hint in the direction of examining not just outward thought or speech but also the sin present within us. Luther also used the language of vice for confession in his *Personal Prayer Book* and consistently used vice terms to describe sin in the Large Catechism.[13]

In fact, Luther wrote his own brief prayer of confession where he guides us to confess in this spirit:

> I confess before God and you that I am a miserable sinner, guilty of every sin, of *unbelief* and of blasphemy. I also feel that God's Word is not bringing forth fruit in me. I hear it, but I do not receive it earnestly. I do not show works of love toward my neighbor. I am full of *anger*, hate, and *envy* toward him. I am impatient, *greedy*, and bent on every evil. Therefore, my heart and conscience are heavy, and I would gladly be freed of my sins. I ask you to strengthen my little faith and comfort my weak conscience by the divine word and promise.[14]

Perhaps most insightful for Luther's practice is this glimpse into his personal self-examination. He remarked to a friend, "I am free from avarice, my age and bodily weakness protect me from sensual desire, and I am not afflicted with hate or envy toward anybody. Up to now, only anger remains in me."[15] Here, Luther used vice categories to confess his own inner struggles.

Praying for Virtue

Examining our sin at the inner level of the heart, where vice resides, inevitably shows us our great need. In these moments,

Luther urged the believer to call upon God, who

> hears most of all when you are in the greatest
> need and fear. Why then are you so foolish in this
> instance, where there is immeasurably greater
> need and eternal hurt, that you do not ask for faith,
> hope, love, patience, obedience, chastity, gentle-
> ness, peace, and righteousness, unless you are
> already free from unbelief, doubt, pride, disobedi-
> ence, unchastity, anger, covetousness, and unrigh-
> teousness? Well then, the more you find yourself
> lacking in these things, the more ought you dili-
> gently to pray and cry unto God.[16]

Thus, the second habit Luther recommended is to pray for the virtue necessary to combat our particular vices.

In his *Personal Prayer Book*, Luther shows us a model of such a prayer, which asks both for deliverance from vice and for the cultivation of virtue. Consider the wealth of vice and virtue language in this single prayer:

> Protect us from unbelief, despair, and from bound-
> less *envy*. Deliver us from the filthy *lust of unchas-
> tity* and grant us a love of every kind of virginity
> and *chastity*. Deliver us from discord, war, and
> dissension, and let the *virtue, peace*, harmony, and
> tranquility of your kingdom draw near. Grant that
> *anger* or other bitterness does not reign over us,
> but that by your grace, genuine *kindness*, loyalty,

and every kind of friendliness, *generosity*, and *gentleness* may reign in us. Grant that inordinate sadness and depression may not prevail in us, but let joy and delight in your grace and mercy come over us.

And finally may *envy* be averted from us and, being filled with your grace and with all *virtues and good deeds*, may we become your kingdom so that in heart, feeling, and thought we may serve you with all our strength inwardly and outwardly, obediently serving your purpose, being governed by you alone and never following self-love, the flesh, the world, or the devil.

Grant that your kingdom, begun in us, may daily increase and improve, lest cunning malice and apathy for doing good overcome us so that we slip back. Rather grant us both earnestly to resolve and to be able to make a beginning to live a pious life as well as to *make vigorous progress in it and reach its goal*. As the prophet says, "Lighten my eyes, lest I sleep the sleep of death or become *slothful* in the good life I have begun, lest my enemy say, 'I have prevailed over him.'"[17]

Later in the *Personal Prayer Book*, we find petitions specifically asking for protection from vice, which Luther grounded in our Baptism: "Help us renounce and forsake the world's deceit and delusion, allurements and fickleness—all its good or evil, *as we vowed to do in baptism.* Help that we may remain steadfast and grow in [the promise of our baptism] from day to day."[18]

The task of the Christian life, at least in part, entails active prayer for and pursuit of virtuous living. In doing so, our hearts are freed from the vices that idolatrously cling to the self and the things of this world so that we can instead serve our neighbor in love—obediently living out the good works God has commanded. In the "Prayer" section at the end of this book, I have included an example of how we might pray for this, using language from the Small Catechism and Scripture.

One helpful analogy for the task of sanctification is tending a garden: in the garden of our soul, we daily cultivate the fruits of faith by the power of the Spirit, pruning sin and pulling the weeds of vice—all so that the faith that has been planted in our heart might thrive and bear abundant fruit. This was a familiar picture offered in the Middle Ages, especially in the realm of vice and virtue.[19]

Luther used similar language of rooting out vice. Discussing the Fifth Commandment, he wrote that "God wants to *remove the root and source* by which the heart is embittered against our neighbor" and encouraged Christians to "learn to calm our wrath and to have a patient, gentle heart." He also said that the Ninth and Tenth Commandments are "especially directed against envy and miserable greed," for "God wants to remove all causes and sources from which arises everything by which we harm our neighbor."[20] And in discussing the Third Petition of the Lord's Prayer, Luther noted,

> Therefore, nothing is more necessary than that we should continually turn towards God's ear, call upon Him, and pray to Him. We must pray that He would give, preserve, and increase faith in us and the fulfillment of the Ten Commandments. . . . We pray that He would *remove everything that is in our way and that opposes us in these matters.*[21]

This imagery coincides with Jesus' parable of the sower, where He compares the word of the kingdom of heaven to seeds sown in various kinds of soil (see Matthew 13:1–9, 18–23). When the seed takes root in good soil, it bears fruit, the desired outcome of our Christian life. But Jesus warns that faith can be choked out by "the cares of the world and the deceitfulness of riches . . . and it proves unfruitful" (Matthew 13:22). In other words, if we do not diligently weed out sinful vices but rather allow them to grow and thrive, our lives will not bear the fruit of faith and we risk our faith entirely.

Therefore, we continuously pray for virtue, for the fruit of the Spirit to grow in us and overflow in love for God and acts of love toward our neighbor.

Progress in the Christian Life

Encouraging Christians to do battle against vice by cultivating virtue inevitably raises questions about making progress in our sanctification. Because, as Luther taught, we can never fully conquer our sin in this life, we might be tempted to think that making progress toward holiness doesn't matter.

But Luther said that Christians must "begin every day and make progress" and "grow day by day in good works," following the words of Paul in 1 Timothy 4:15: "Practice these things, immerse yourself in them, so that all may see your progress." Our sinful nature rises each day, but as we continue to fight against it, the "poison decreases more and more from day to day and we always wipe out, wash, and cleanse the poison, with the poison becoming less." Elsewhere, Luther noted the importance of vice and virtue in this fight: "The virtues do not ascend unless our weaknesses also descend. The ascent and the descent takes place at the same time, that is, the increase of virtues and of humility." We will never completely eradicate the poison of sin in us in this life, but "God's kingdom does indeed begin and grow here . . . [and] it will be perfected in yonder life."[22]

Luther used Jesus' brief parable of the leaven in Matthew 13:33 to describe the gradual process of sanctification:

> The new leaven is the faith and grace of the Spirit. It does not leaven the whole lump at once but gently, and gradually, we become like this new leaven and eventually, a bread of God. This life, therefore, is not godliness but the process of becoming godly, not health but getting well, not being but becoming, not rest but exercise. We are not now what we shall be, but we are on the way. The process is not yet finished, but it is actively going on. This is not the goal but it is the right road. At present,

everything does not gleam and sparkle, but everything is being cleansed.[23]

Sanctification is not an option for Christians; it is essential.
We must engage in this fight. Hear the steady drumbeat of Luther,
summoning us to battle:

- There is no condemnation *if they fight against themselves
  and their sin.*

- Sin does not impair our salvation, *provided we fight
  against it and do not surrender.*

- God does not hold against us whatever sin is still to
  be driven out . . . *because of our steady battle against sin*
  which we continue to expel.

- [God] has promised mercy and forgiveness to all who,
  at the very least, do not consent to this part of themselves but *fight against it* and are *eager to annihilate it.*[24]

Echoing Paul's argument in Romans 6, Luther wrote:

Christ did not come that you might remain in your
sin and in condemnation. You will not be saved
unless you stop your sinning. . . . You must cease
your covetousness, adultery, and fornication. . . .
Wherever faith is genuine, there is no love for sin.
Nor does a true believer remain in sin, but he shuns
it. . . . Therefore see to it that you avoid . . . open
vices and sins.[25]

Again, we do this imperfectly, and God's mercy abounds in Christ. What matters is that we live out our Baptism by *engaging* in the fight against sin, for we show that we have "been made a Christian by love and good works and [fleeing] all vices."[26]

As long as there is struggle, faith can exist, regardless of relative progress. In fact, Christians will likely experience seasons of apparent regress. This in itself is not evidence that faith is absent. But if we abandon the fight entirely? That is a sure sign that faith has been lost. Luther summed up our ongoing participation in the fight of faith with the first of his Ninety-Five Theses: "When our Lord and Master Jesus Christ said, 'Repent' [Matt. 4:17], he willed the entire life of believers to be one of repentance."[27]

Only God's merciful declaration can make us righteous in God's eyes, and in this respect, humans are truly passive and do nothing to contribute to our salvation. However, when we reject God's design for our life and pursue habits of unbelief by living in vice, we erode our faith and trust in God's mercy. In time, the link we have to God by grace could be fully severed by our stubborn and persistent unrepentance, which refuses to trust in God and to live accordingly. Luther understood this reality and therefore exhorted Christians to diligently live out our faith, daily confessing and fleeing vice and praying for Christian virtue to rise in its place.

A Church Clothed in Christ

Despite his misgivings about Aristotle and the tradition of virtue ethics in the church, Luther worked to reform our understanding of these concepts for use in Christian life. He drew heavily on the vice tradition to develop his understanding of sin, but he redefined virtue according to the fruit of the Spirit, pointing to the Decalogue as the primary guide for living out our faith. Luther specifically highlighted the movement from vice to virtue as a hallmark of genuine Christianity and a way to identify the church:

> The Holy Spirit sanctifies us . . . when we bear no one a grudge, entertain no anger, hatred, envy, or vengefulness toward our neighbors, but gladly forgive them, lend to them, help them, and counsel them; when we are not lewd, not drunkards, not proud, arrogant, overbearing, but chaste, self-controlled, sober, friendly, kind, gentle, and humble; when we do not steal, rob, are not usurious, greedy, do not overcharge, but are mild, kind, content, charitable; when we are not false, mendacious, perjurers, but truthful, trustworthy, and do whatever else is taught in these commandments. . . . Thus we must constantly grow in sanctification and always become new creatures in Christ.[28]

I pray Luther's insights into vice and virtue, especially as he described the task of what it means to live baptized, will equip you as you engage in the battle of your soul. In closing, I offer a description of the church from Luther's commentary on Psalm 90:

> The church is made up of those who move forward in the process of sanctification, who day by day "put off the old and put on the new man."[29]

While this may not sound like the Luther we thought we knew, his words ring true. Dressed in our Baptism, God's people endeavor to kill our unbelief and allow the new man to emerge each day by fighting the good fight of faith.

Today is another day God has granted you life, breath, and being. Today is another day you have awakened as a baptized child of God. It's time to go out into the world. What will you wear today?

> For as many of you as were baptized in Christ
> have put on Christ.
>
> (*Galatians 3:27*)

EPILOGUE

RETURNING TO BAPTISM

Luther and others of his day who were raised in the church had a very different understanding of the benefits of Baptism than what Luther would eventually teach. Luther "had been raised to regard Baptism as being very limited in its benefits."[1] The Roman Catholic Church taught that, while Baptism purified an individual from original sin, it did not provide any benefit for subsequent sins. Thus, most people did not think Baptism had any real saving benefit, because people inevitably continue to sin, and the promise of Baptism would soon be nullified.

Luther later worked to correct this misunderstanding and restore the full comfort and promises of Baptism to Christians. He wrote in the Large Catechism:

> [I must] correct the opinion, which has long prevailed among us, that baptism is something past that we can no longer use after falling back into sin. This idea comes from looking only at the act that took place a single time. Indeed, St. Jerome is responsible for this view, for he wrote, "Penance is the second plank on which we must swim ashore after the ship founders," [the ship] in which we embarked when we entered the Christian community. This takes away the value of baptism, making it of no further use to us. Therefore it is incorrect to say this. The ship does not break up because . . . it is God's ordinance and not something that is ours. But it does happen that we slip and fall out of the

ship. However, those who do fall out should immediately see to it that they swim to the ship and hold
fast to it, until they can climb aboard again and sail
on it as before.[2]

Jerome and subsequently the Roman Church taught that Baptism was the "first plank" by which we enter the church. However, they also taught that our persistent sin can destroy the ship of our salvation, leaving us floundering. The only way for our faith to survive was to cling to the remnants of the ship, floating to safety by grabbing the "second plank" of penance for our sins. Paul does teach in 1 Timothy 1:19 that it is possible for Christians to make "shipwreck of their faith" by rejecting it. But Luther emphasized that

> Baptism is an unsinkable ship. Intentional,
> persistent post-baptismal sin does not destroy
> the ship of Baptism, but rather causes you to fall
> overboard. Repentance, in Luther's view, is how
> you hold on to the ship until you can climb back
> onboard.[3]

One way to comprehend the daily task of the baptized is to think of it as swimming back to the ship, back to the promise of our Baptism. When we fall away from that promise because of our unrepentant sin, God has not abandoned His own promise made to us at the font. The strong ship of salvation He has won for us sails on! But we will most certainly drown if we do not endeavor, in the power of the Spirit, to make our way back to the ship. That's what true repentance is: returning to the safety of the ship of our salvation, returning to our Baptism.

Through repentance, we daily drown our sinful nature and its vices, and our new self in Christ rises, holding fast to this strong ship so that we might remain partakers in the promise of salvation that our Baptism continually offers us. May the Spirit grant you the strength to keep on returning to your Baptism and clinging tightly to its benefits until that day when, with all the faithful on board, you at last reach the heavenly shore, safe and secure forever.

PRAYERS

Prayer of Confession

Father in heaven, I confess to You the evil thoughts that come from within me, out of my unclean heart. Forgive my envy—the times when I begrudge the generosity You show to others and find joy in their sorrows. Forgive my greed—when I seek security in the abundance of my possessions and ignore my neighbor in need. Forgive my lust—the times when I look at another with adulterous eyes, seeking personal pleasure and sexual gratification. Forgive my gluttony—when I attempt to live by bread alone and not by every word that proceeds from Your mouth. Forgive my anger—when I seek to avenge injustice by hating my enemies instead of producing the righteousness that You desire. Forgive my slothfulness—the times when I am indifferent to the call of Your Word and neglect to walk in the good works You have prepared for me. Father, forgive my prideful heart, which seeks to displace You as the rightful Lord of my life instead of being Your humble servant. Remind me of my Savior, Jesus Christ, who was delivered up for my trespasses and raised for my justification. Grant to me a new heart and put a new Spirit within me. Remove my heart of stone and give me a heart of flesh. Forgive me for all my sins, that I might live in Your holy peace. Amen.

Scripture used in this prayer: Mark 7:21–22; Matthew 20:15; Luke 12:15; Matthew 5:28; 4:4; 5:22; Romans 12:19; James 1:20; Ephesians 2:10; Matthew 25:31–46; 20:26; Philippians 2:3–7; James 4:6–10; Romans 4:25; Ezekiel 36:26.

Prayer for the Fruit of the Spirit

Lord, grow in me the fruit of the Spirit, that I might lovingly walk in the good works You have prepared for me. Grant me kindness, so that I will steadfastly uphold the reputation of others by defending them, speaking well of them, and explaining everything in the kindest way. Grant me goodness, that I might generously give to my neighbors in need and help them improve and protect their possessions and income. Grant me self-control, that I might shun the passions of the flesh which wage war against my soul and that I might lead a sexually pure and decent life in all I say and do. Grant me gentleness and peace, that I might help and support the needs of my neighbor and forgive others as You have forgiven me. Grant me patience, that I might bear with those in authority over me, that I would honor them, serve and obey them, and love and cherish them. Grant me joy in my callings, that I might diligently serve You and my neighbor in love and that I would continue to hold Your Word sacred and gladly hear and learn it. Grant me faithfulness, that in humility I might not consider equality with God a thing to be grasped, but would fear, love, and trust in You above all things. Lord, give me strength to abide in Your baptismal promise and so bear abundant fruit. Empower me with the love You pour into my heart through the Holy Spirit whom You have given to me. Amen.

Scripture used in this prayer: Galatians 5:22–23; Ephesians 2:10; Philippians 2:3–7; John 15:5; Romans 5:5.

VICES AS MANIFESTATIONS OF UNBELIEF

COVETOUS VICE	FEAR (Lack of trust *leads to* sinful desire)		LOVE (Disordered love (Augustine, Aquinas))		TRUST (Root in pride *equals* unbelief (Luther))	CONTRARY VIRTUE
	I fear ...	I desire ...				
PRIDE	... I'm not valued	... to prove my worth	I love myself, so I serve my interests above all others	**Perverted Love** (*Pursuing otherwise worthy goals in a misguided manner*)	**I assume the place of God** (*Trust in myself*)	HUMILITY
ENVY	... I'll have it worse than others	... to improve my status	I love my reputation, so I manipulate my social standing			KINDNESS
ANGER	... there won't be justice	... to enact justice	I love justice, so I avenge wrongdoing in God's stead			PATIENCE
SLOTH	... my obligations are too burdensome	... to be free of responsibility	I neglect to walk in the good works God has prepared for me	**Indifferent Love**	**I spurn the call to love God** and serve others	DILIGENCE
GREED	... I won't have enough	... to have more	I seek self-security and thus love possessions of this world in a disordered manner	**Excessive Love** (*Loving otherwise good gifts of creation too much*)	**I replace God** with created things (*Trust in the things of this world*)	GENEROSITY
GLUTTONY	... I'll feel empty	... to be physically fulfilled	I seek self-satisfaction and thus love pleasures of this world in a disordered manner			TEMPERANCE
LUST	... I'll be alone					CHASTITY

Idolatry/Unbelief

ACKNOWLEDGMENTS

My sincere thanks to the professionals at Concordia Publishing House for their patience and willingness to partner with a first-time author. The entire team played a pivotal role in bringing this volume to publication, but none more so than my editor, Jamie Moldenhauer. Her expertise helped transform a manuscript originally written for academic purposes into a book that is certain to connect with any Christian.

I am especially indebted to the faculty of Concordia Seminary—and particularly the team who supervised my doctoral dissertation, of which this text is an adaptation. Thanks to my dissertation readers, Dr. Erik Herrmann and Dr. Robert Kolb, for their insights. These men challenged me to think through the implications of my research more clearly, enhancing the manner in which they have been presented. Special thanks to my adviser, Dr. Joel Biermann, both for his guidance during my graduate studies and also for encouraging me to reshape my work into a format that would be more accessible to lay readers—that they would be more likely to encounter its content, might more readily grasp its teachings, and thus might be further formed in their Christian faith. His continued support has been a most welcome gift.

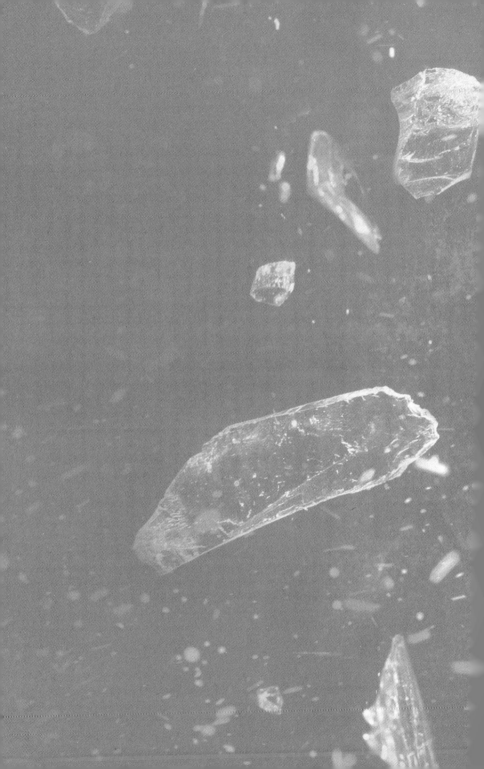

NOTES

Preface

1   Small Catechism, Baptism, Second Part.

2   Small Catechism, Baptism, Fourth Part.

3   Kolb-Wengert, LC IV 65–68, emphasis added.

Introduction

1   LW 34:337.

2   LW 31:12.

Part 1

1   Luther quotations in this section are from LW 27:289; 32:20, emphasis and brackets added.

Chapter 1

1   *Lutheran Service Book*, p. 151, emphasis added.

2   Luther quotations in this paragraph are from LW 34:114; 32:224, brackets added.

3   LW 32:220–21.

4   LW 44:114.

5   Luther quotations in this paragraph are from LW 32:25, 19, 27, emphasis and brackets added.

6   See Karl Barth, *Church Dogmatics*, vol. 4, *The Doctrine of Reconciliation* (New York: T&T Clark, 1961), 253.

7   LW 32:209. See also LW 32:28; 34:190.

8   Luther quotations in this paragraph are from LW 36:210, 204.

9   See LW 36:209–10.

10   LW 34:186–87.

11   Luther quotes in this paragraph are from LW 34:182.

Chapter 2

1   LC I 12.

2   See LW 44:109.

3   LW 29:154.

4   See *Purgatorio*, canto 17, 85–139, especially 94–96.

5   Quotes in this paragraph are from LW 44:30; 43:21, emphasis added.

6   LC I 2–3.

7   Quotes in this paragraph are from LW 44:108, brackets added; 45:336.

8   Quotes in this paragraph are from LW 29:154, emphasis added; 31:350; 29:155.

9   LW 51:138–39.

Chapter 3

1   See Kostya Kennedy et al., "Billy Joel: 50 Years of the Piano Man," *Life*, September 2, 2022, 30–34.

2   See Evagrius, *Eight Evil Thoughts*, and *The Praktikos*, 6.

3   Quotes in this paragraph are from LW 25:160; 34:154.

4   Quotes in this paragraph are from LW 11:259, brackets added; 28:340; 8:56.

5   Quotes in this paragraph are from LW 32:207, 216; 41:18.

6   LC III 102–3.

7   Quotes in this paragraph are from LW 12:207; 25:319.

8   LW 32:253.

Chapter 4

1   See LW 27:84.

2   Quotes in this paragraph are from LW 34:144; 42:40; 3:22.

3   LW 27:172.

4   Quotes in this paragraph are from LW 44:87; 29:155.

5   Quotes in this paragraph are from LW 44:30; 27:58.

6   LW 3:25–26.

7   LW 27:93, emphasis added.

8   LW 42:28, emphasis added.

9   LC I 195, emphasis added.

10 See LC I 313.

Chapter 5

1   Quotes in this paragraph are from Kolb-Wengert, LC VI 1–4; LW 39:28.

2   Quotes in this paragraph are from LW 39:37; 43:12.

3   Quotes in this paragraph are from LW 43:14; 39:37; 43:21.

4   See LW 39:33–34.

5   LW 39:37–38, emphasis added.

6   LW 44:23.

7   LW 43:23–24.

8   LW 31:364–65.

9   Albrecht Peters, *Ten Commandments*, 96.

10 See LC I 195.

Chapter 6

1   Gregory, *Moralia* 31.45.87 (Oxford: John Henry Parker; London: J. G. F. and J. Rivington, 1844; Lectionary Central), http://www.lectionarycentral.com /gregorymoraliaindex.html (accessed May 9, 2023).

2   LW 40:274, emphasis added.

3   Quotations in this paragraph are from LW 34:183; 44:113.

4   See LW 34:176.

5   LC Preface 5.

6   LW 41:114.

7   LW 32:28, 29.

8   LC III 104–5.

9   Quotes in this paragraph are from LW 44:106, 49.

10 Quotes in this paragraph are from LW 44:74, 72–73, emphasis added.

11 LW 42:44.

12 LW 32:20, 22, emphasis added.

13 See LW 27:65–67.

14 LW 26:220, brackets and emphasis added.

15 LW 27:48, 65, emphasis added.

16 See LW 32:229; 35:369–70.

17 LW 41:114

18 See LW 32:229.

Part 2

1   Luther quotations in this section are from LW 32:24.

Chapter 7

1   LC I 256.

2   LC I 263.

3   Quotations in this paragraph are from LC I 266, 276, 273, brackets added.

4   LC I 285.

5   LC I 184, emphasis added.

6   See Thomas Aquinas, *Summa Theologiae* II–II.36.1.

7   LC I 307, emphasis added.

8   Quotations in this paragraph are from Kolb-Wengert, LC I 264, 267–68.

9   LW 29:77.

10   Quotations in this paragraph are from LW 30:118; 27:94, emphasis added.

11   LW 29:76–77, brackets added.

Chapter 8

1   See LC I 225.

2   Quotations in this paragraph are from LC I 224; LW 43:23 (see also LW 43:20 for another list of activities Luther saw as breaking the principle of the Seventh Commandment); LC I 227, 233.

3   See LW 24:162.

4   Peters, *Ten Commandments*, 266.

5   See Aquinas, *Summa Theologiae* II–II.118.2.

6   LW 44:108.

7   LW 44:107. See also LC I 7.

8   See Ricardo Rieth, "Luther on Greed," in *Harvesting Martin Luther's Reflections on Theology, Ethics, and the Church*, ed. Timothy J. Wengert (Minneapolis, MN: Fortress Press, 2017), 152–68.

9   LW 19:187, 202, emphasis added.

10 LC I 43.

11 LW 45:317–18.

12 LW 45:248.

13 See Robert Kolb, *Luther's Treatise* On Christian Freedom *and Its Legacy* (New York: Lexington/Fortress Press, 2020), 76.

14 LW 21:189.

15 LW 44:108. See LW 27:94; 29:79.

16 Quotations in this paragraph are from LW 43:23; Kolb-Wengert, LC I 246; LC I 249.

17 See Rieth, "Luther on Greed."

18 Quotations in this paragraph are from LW 21:194, 201.

Chapter 9

1 Quotations in this paragraph are from LC I 200, 202.

2 See LW 43:19–20.

3 LC I 206–8.

4 Quotations in this paragraph are from Smalcald Articles III XI 2; Augsburg Confession XXIII 1, brackets added.

5 See LC I 211–12; Peters, *Ten Commandments*, 243.

6 LW 44:104.

7 See Evagrius, *Eight Evil Thoughts* 1.11.

8   LW 30:250.

9   See Aquinas, *Summa Theologiae* II–II.148.1.

10 See Gregory, *Moralia* 30.18.

11 LW 25:482.

12 LW 30:27, brackets added.

13 Quotations in this paragraph are from LW 44:106, 104.

14 LW 27:95, brackets added.

15 LW 27:378.

Chapter 10

1   LC I 182, brackets added.

2   Peters, *Ten Commandments*, 226.

3   LC I 184, 186, brackets added.

4   Quotations in this paragraph are from LC I 189 and the Small Catechism, explanation of the Fifth Commandment.

5   LC I 105.

6   Small Catechism, explanation of the Fourth Commandment.

7   Quotations in this paragraph are from LW 44:80–81; LC I 150.

8   LW 40:283.

9   LW 45:62–63.

10 LW 45:111–12.

11 *What Luther Says* § 80.

12 See Aquinas, *Summa Theologiae* II–II.158.2–3.

13 LW 31:306.

14 Jeffrey Gibbs, "The Myth of 'Righteous Anger': What the Bible Says About Human Anger," *Concordia Pages*, November 27, 2018, 16, https://concordiatheology.org/2018/11/jeff-gibbs-the-myth-of-righteous-anger/.

15 Quotations in this paragraph are from LC I 182, 181, brackets added.

16 See LW 46:93–137.

17 LW 45:100.

18 LW 44:101.

19 LC I 187.

20 LC I 195, emphasis added.

21 LW 40:281.

22 Quotations in this paragraph are from LW 27:94–95.

23 LW 42:66, brackets added.

Chapter 11

1 See LC I 82.

2 Small Catechism, explanation of the Third Commandment.

3 Quotations in this paragraph are from LC I 90, 84, 87–88.

4 LC I 91–92.

5 Kolb-Wengert, LC I 98–99.

6   LW 54:281.

7   Dorothy L. Sayers, *Letters to a Diminished Church* (Nashville, TN: Thomas Nelson, 2004), 97.

8   LW 6:362.

9   LW 29:153–54, emphasis added.

10 Quotations in this paragraph are from LW 42:62; Kolb-Wengert, LC III 67, brackets added.

11 LW 13:176, emphasis added.

12 LW 44:34.

13 LC I 100–101.

Chapter 12

1   LW 2:125–26.

2   LW 44:42.

3   Quotations in this paragraph are from LW 44:43.

4   LW 32:91.

5   Quotations in this paragraph are from LW 44:43; 30:250.

6   LW 44:25.

7   LW 31:302.

8   LW 31:365–66.

9   See Kolb, *Luther's Treatise* On Christian Freedom, 64.

10 LW 31:366.

Conclusion

1 Kolb-Wengert, LC IV 84, emphasis added.

2 Kolb-Wengert, LC IV 85.

3 Quotes in this paragraph are from the Solid Declaration VI 4, emphasis added.

4 Kolb-Wengert, Epitome IV 18, brackets added.

5 Quotations in this paragraph are from LC I 75, 332; LW 44:109.

6 Quotations in this paragraph are from LC Short Preface 4; I 75.

7 LW 44:102.

8 LC I 47.

9 Small Catechism, Baptism, Fourth Part.

10 LW 44:63, emphasis added.

11 LW 40:276.

12 *Lutheran Service Book*, p. 151.

13 Quotations in this paragraph are from the Small Catechism, Confession, "Which are these?"

For examples of confessing vice in the *Personal Prayer Book*, see LW 43:16, 19, 20. For references to the seven capital vices in the Large Catechism, see the Kolb-Wengert edition as follows: *pride* (LC I 38; II 21; III 90, 103); *envy* (LC I 184, 307–10; III 43, 103); *anger* (LC I 182, 185–86; III 103); *sloth* (LC Preface 1, 4, 9; I 96–99; II 67, 102); *greed* (LC I 43, 96, 243, 307; II 21); *gluttony* (LC Preface 2; I 96; II 43; III 102); *lust* (LC I 201, 215; III, 43, 102).

202

14 LW 53:117–18, emphasis added.

15 LW 54:26–27.

16 LW 44:64.

17 LW 43:32, emphasis added.

18 LW 43:37, emphasis added. Brackets in original.

19 This analogy extended to Luther's day as well, such as in the common prayer book *The Garden of the Soul*. Luther criticized this book for its vast enumeration of sins, as discussed in chapter 5, but the general analogy is still beneficial.

20 Quotations in this paragraph are from LC I 187, 310, emphasis added.

21 LC III 2, emphasis added.

22 Luther quotations in this paragraph are from LW 27:169; 34:181, 182; 11:325; 42:40.

23 LW 32:24.

24 Quotations in this list are from LW 32:239, 28, 212, emphasis added.

25 LW 22:389.

26 LW 34:161, emphasis added.

27 LW 31:83.

28 LW 41:166.

29 LW 13:89–90.

Epilogue

1   Benjamin T. G. Mayes, *Martin Luther on Holy Baptism* (St. Louis, MO: Concordia Publishing House, 2018), viii.

2   Kolb-Wengert, LC IV 80–82.

3   Mayes, *Martin Luther on Holy Baptism*, x.

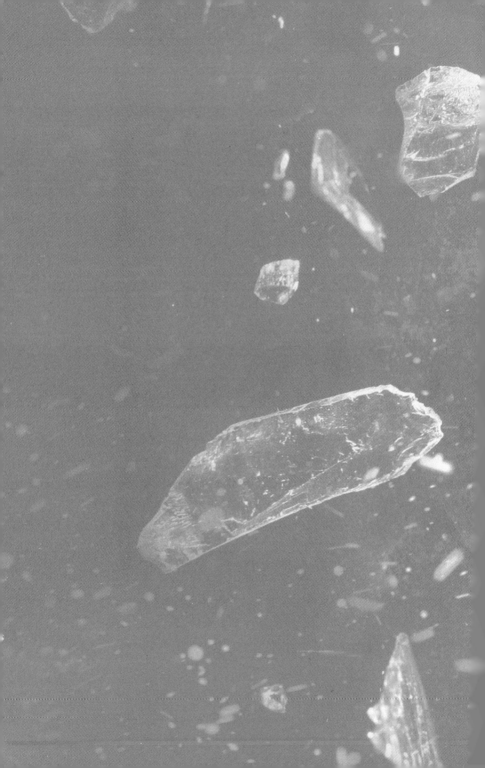